HOW TO PLAN A SUCCESSFUL TRIP

Ellen Hoffman

Farragut Publishing Company
Washington, D.C.
1988

PRINTED IN THE UNITED STATES OF AMERICA

Book design by Eason Associates

Library of Congress Cataloging-in-Publication Data

Hoffman, Ellen, 1943-
    How to plan a successful trip.

    Bibliography: p.
    Includes index.
    1. Travel. I. Title.
G151.H64   1988   910'.2'02   88-11312
ISBN 0-918535-05-0 (pbk.)

To my parents, who always
told me I could do
whatever I wanted to do.

ACKNOWLEDGEMENTS

For their research, advice and counsel, I thank Hilary Freer, Liz Gearhold and Suzanne Singer. My thanks and appreciation are also extended to Maxine Freund and George Idelson, to Dr. Charles Ehret of the Argonne Research Laboratory and Dorothy Jordon of the Travel With Your Children Resource Center as well as to the following organizations: American Association of Retired Persons, American Hotel-Motel Association, American Society of Travel Agents, Council of Better Business Bureaus, and the U.S. Department of Transportation, including the Federal Aviation Administration.

CONTENTS

INTRODUCTION

We had picnicked on the terrace of the 100-year old farmhouse overlooking the Mediterranean. We had hiked along a goat trail to market in a tiny, brilliant white village. We had luxuriated in the aroma of lilacs cascading over the walls of the Alhambra. But my vacation in Spain had now come to an end and it was time to go home.

The Granada airport seemed suspiciously empty, even for a Sunday. We woke the dozing agent at a car rental counter, who delivered the devastating news.

"The flight to Madrid? It left half an hour ago," he informed us. "No, there are no more flights today."

How could I have missed my plane? We had arrived in what we were sure was plenty of time. The answer was deceptively simple: we did not know that overnight Spain had switched to daylight savings time. Failing to pick up that bit of information cost me several hundred dollars and a day away from work.

The only way to reach Madrid, where I was to catch a plane back to the States, was to rent a car, drive hundreds of miles, spend the night in a hotel and wait on stand-by for the next available seat. I obtained one the next day but because I'd missed the return on the proper date, the flight home cost the same as my original round-trip ticket.

Now I always read the airline schedules carefully and

double-check departure and arrival times before I leave home,
and at my destination.

Anticipate the Unexpected

The unexpected can make or break a day or a week or an
entire business trip or vacation.

At their best, travel surprises become the stories told and
retold fondly whenever friends who are travelers congregate.

At their worst, travel surprises are a disaster as well as
a disruption.

The business traveler who misses a flight and therefore
an important meeting may feel he or she has been dealt a
genuine disaster. The retired couple who pinched pennies
to finance their first trip overseas might feel the same way
when one of them becomes ill and the trip is cut short.

In recent years we Americans have been setting records
for the frequency and extent of our travels. We take more
weekend trips, we take more business trips, and we combine
more business trips with pleasure than in the past. People
with special needs—e.g., senior citizens and the handicapped—who found travel difficult or impossible in the past—
are now striking out in greater numbers than ever before.

At the same time, the effects of airline deregulation have
been taking their toll in confusion, delayed flights, lost time,
stress and concerns about safety. We travel more, but whether
we enjoy it more is debatable.

Some of us travel because we have to; others because we
want to. But all travelers have this in common: Distant from
the resources and moral support of the home, family and
office, we rightfully feel vulnerable. What might be minor
dislocations and frustrations at home turn into disasters.

What can you do to prevent such disasters?

Anticipate the unexpected.

That's what this book is about.

The Decision Chain

What is a successful trip? It's one on which you accom-
plish your own goals of business or pleasure—getting the
contract, becoming re-acquainted with old friends, climb-

ing a mountain—with a minimum of hassle and stress.

Planning and taking a successful trip can be viewed as a series of decisions. Where to go, when to go, with whom, how to get there, what to take must all be confronted before departure. There is no choice. Some other decisions—such as whether to spend an extra day on the beach, or to change the itinerary so you can spend time with new-found friends, can be made en route.

But for most of us, the more unexpected decisions we have to confront en route, the more stressful travel becomes. Changes in travel arrangements often require information not available on the road. In foreign countries, telephone calls and language barriers can add to the difficulties.

More than ever, advance thinking and planning are the most important ingredients in making your trip a success. They are particularly important for the business traveler for whom time is money; and for vacationers bound to a fixed itinerary and date of return.

Thinking Ahead

The more preparations you make ahead of time, the better off you'll be on your next trip.

This doesn't mean you can't be spontaneous. But even spontaneous travel can be more enjoyable with a bit of advance planning. For example, you can increase the odds of enjoying your vacation by deciding what you want to do before deciding where you want to go. If your eyes glaze after two days of looking at Renaissance art in museums, think carefully before booking a whole week in Florence. If the beach is a necessity for your first three days of vacation and a bore on the fourth, don't lock yourself into two weeks on a desert island.

Avoid the hassles and stress of spontaneous but uninformed changes of plans. If you want to spend a month hopping from one Greek island to another, study a ferry map before you go so that you know if it's even possible to get from here to there. Carry an airline timetable with you, buy a ticket which allows for changes with no or minimum financial penalties, and pack a warm sweater if there's a chance you'll end up in the mountains in October.

A Practical Guide

The purpose of this book is to help you make NECESSARY decisions before you leave, to streamline the process of getting away—regardless of where you are going or why—and to free you from the anxieties and uncertainties which can make you wish you'd never left your doorstep.

Information from a book cannot guarantee that you'll never spend 12 hours stranded in an airport, or never arrive without your luggage, or never be robbed in a strange city. But by starting your trip planning early and following the numerous practical suggestions in this book you can reduce the risk of such occurrences or minimize their effects.

The suggestions come from a journalist and self-taught traveler who has criss-crossed the world on both business and pleasure trips—a traveler who seeks to protect you from information overload and to provide you with tips and tools to make the necessary decisions quickly and efficiently.

The book is organized and designed to assist you in planning a successful journey, regardless of the amount of your travel experience or the purpose, duration or distance of the trip.

If you haven't traveled much, or haven't been out of the U.S., start by skimming all the chapters and then return to them, one by one, as you grapple with specific problems such as how to find the right hotel, what type of luggage to bring, whether to obtain special insurance, and how to ensure that you have the necessary documents before you leave.

If you're an experienced traveler, use this volume as a reference book. For example, if you haven't been overseas lately, refer to the chapter on legal formalities. It will help you remember those critical "details"—to make sure your passport's current, to have passport pictures taken, to give yourself time to apply for visas, and to learn how to avoid excessive customs duties when you return to the U.S.

If you're considering a first-time major vacation with grandparents and children, turn to Chapter Nine, "When a Family Travels," for ideas and resources on how to bridge the generation gaps and plan a congenial, conflict-free trip.

No matter who you are or where you're going, the checklists at the end of each chapter can be used over and over again.

Travelers who have special needs will find tips for them throughout the text and a list of basic resources in the appendices which provide detailed guidance on issues such as services and requirements of airlines for disabled passengers.

Here's where to look for information in this book:

In each chapter, you'll encounter a list of "how-tos" to consider before you go on a trip—questions to ask yourself to help plan, and the steps to take.

The appendices contain lists of free or low-cost publications or other information on questions such as how to pack, your legal rights as a traveler, and how to choose a hotel, as well as general publications which address a range of travel planning issues.

And at the end of the book you'll find a "Traveler's Personal Data Card" to fill out and take along to ensure that you have all the necessary phone numbers, travelers check numbers and other data to help you get through unexpected emergencies on your next trip.

When you follow the advice in this book it will help you in two ways:

- To avoid hassles and irritations by providing for your comfort and your needs ahead of time; and

- To relax or concentrate—or both—whether on closing a business deal or on having fun. Equipped with tickets, hotel reservations, the proper clothing and some handy information which will help if problems present themselves en route you'll lose less sleep and less time.

What's more, using this book will lighten your load. Because this is one travel guide you can leave at home.

Chapter One

MAKING RESERVATIONS: WITH OR WITHOUT A TRAVEL AGENT

The peaked roof of the wooden cabin sloped nearly to the ground. Through a fringe of tropical foliage, from the front window we could gaze at the tranquil blue-gray-green surface of Lake Toba not far below.

For breakfast we dined on banana pancakes while sitting on a balcony from which pink and red bougainvillea cascaded toward the lakeshore.

The "Carolina Losmen" on the Indonesian island of Samosir is a hotel you'll never be able to book through a travel agent, but it's one of the most memorable places this traveler has ever slept (especially for $1.25 a night).

Sometimes the best part of a trip is not knowing where you'll sleep tomorrow night or whether you'll arrive at the next destination by train or plane.

This represents the ultimate luxury in travel—when the voyager has time to burn, to experiment and to be free of rigid itineraries and reservations.

Most travelers, however, lack that luxury, and some of us are constitutionally incapable of relaxing and enjoying a trip which is fraught with uncertainties. Thus both vacation and business travelers constantly confront the problem of how to book hotels and transportation for their next trip.

Computerization theoretically has brought efficiency and

information to the fingertips of every travel agent and airlines reservations clerk. But—along with airline deregulation—computerization seems to have provoked an explosion in the number of travel options from which we have to choose. Sunday travel sections bristle with ads for "bargains" and the morning paper bombards us with full-page, big-print announcements of the latest "super-maxi-ultimate-saver" air fares and tour packages.

What is the most efficient way for a traveler to navigate through the maze of air fares and special packages, or to book a room at an appropriate hotel in an unfamiliar destination? In the past the primary answer to this question has been: Use a travel agent or an airline reservations agent. And now there is a third possibility as well—using your own computer.

This chapter will lay out the pros and cons of each method and reduce frustration and hassles by clarifying your own responsibility as a traveler for making travel arrangements.

Booking Through a Travel Agent

What a travel agent can do for you: A travel agent can reserve accommodations, transportation, special travel packages or tours which might include both of these elements, provide information about your options and assist you in preparations for the trip (e.g., passport and health requirements, etc.).

What a travel agent can't do for you: A travel agent cannot decide where you should take your vacation if you have no idea what you want out of it. An agent can't figure out which hotel to book you in unless you know what type of location you seek, what you can pay and what services you require.

Seek out an agent if you are planning a complicated trip—whether to a new destination or an old one—for which you'll need expert advice on subjects such as the best airline connections or how to minimize costs or time spent in moving from place to place. Also use one when you require special facilities or accommodations—for the business traveler, perhaps, a computer in the hotel room; for the vacationer, accessibility to a golf course.

Be aware that there is a difference between using a travel agency in general and a particular agent.

Try to develop a personal relationship with an individual agent and rely on him or her for continuing advice on where to go, when to go and how to go—as well as to book your trips. An advantage of this is that you'll be spared the necessity of reiterating your personal travel needs and preferences to a new person every time you go out of town. Your agent can short-cut travel planning time by keeping a file on you which includes information such as seating and meal preferences on airplanes, which class you prefer to travel and frequent flyer club memberships.

If your regular agent is out of town or unavailable, theoretically the travel agency should be able to offer an equally effective substitute. But the reality is that you're likely to receive much better service from the individual who knows you and who can rely on receiving your future business.

To find a travel agent, as in almost any business, a reference from a satisfied customer who happens to be your friend or colleague is the best bet. Some agencies specialize in either business or vacation travel. Others specialize in arranging trips to domestic destinations, others to Europe, still others to more exotic places. Others may specialize in cruises or skiing expeditions. Often the ads in the yellow pages can guide you to these specialists. If you already know an agent who handles your business travel, consider giving your personal business to that same agent.

In addition to the above criteria, you may want to check on whether your proposed travel agent is a C.T.C. or a member of ASTA or ARTA. C.T.C. stands for "certified travel counselor," a designation awarded to travel agents with at least five years' experience who have completed a two- to three-year course of study at the Institute of Certified Travel Agents. Award of the certification carries with it an obligation to a professional code of ethics which prohibits use of improper sales techniques, misleading advertising and other undesirable practices.

The American Society of Travel Agents (ASTA) and the Association of Retail Travel Agents (ARTA) also require their members to meet certain business and professional standards. ASTA members are expected to comply with certain "principles of professional conduct and ethics" including providing factual information, details about the conditions of any travel products bought and confidentiality. ARTA has a code of responsibility as well, but unlike ASTA, no disciplinary procedures for violators. (See Chapter Ten, "Your Rights as a Travel Consumer," for information on grievance procedures.)

Travel agents garner their income from commissions for bookings. Although there may be some variations, rates tend to be about 12 percent for an international flight, 10 percent for a domestic flight and 10 percent for a hotel, according to ASTA.

Thus as airline fare wars escalate, travel agents' commissions decline. And as the number of complicated airfares in the market increases, the incentive for an agent to sort them out for you decreases.

In general, travel agents have less incentive to spend their time assisting an individual traveler—especially if that person is committed to bargain-hunting. That's why you might receive better service if you or your office has a business account with the same agency.

Some travel agencies charge fees for their services—e.g., a flat rate for issuing an airline ticket. If you're in doubt about whether you'll be charged, be sure to ask. If an agency makes an international call or sends a cable on your behalf, you are likely to be charged for the costs.

Booking Through Airlines

Although it's well known that many airlines will book package tours, it's less known that sometimes you can reserve a hotel room through the same agent who books your seat on a plane.

Often the business traveler who, for example, simply needs a hotel for five nights, will find that the airline can reserve it through the computerized system. Another time to consider booking a hotel through the airline is when you're arriving in an unfamiliar destination and just need a room for the first night.

Some airlines have "partner" hotels and only list those hotels or chains in their computers. Others offer a range of options. Both Japan Airlines and Swissair, for example, can book a variety of accommodations for you in all the cities on their routes. If you know the name of the hotel you want and it's not in the computer system, some airlines will request it and call you back to confirm later. (Some offer the same service for car rentals.) When you book through an airline, you'll probably receive a confirmation number but not a piece of paper to present to the hotel on your arrival.

The advantages of booking through an airline are: it's a one-stop transaction; availability is usually known instantly; and in some cases you'll save the cost of phone calls or cables for which you might be billed by a travel agent. Most major airlines have a toll-free telephone reservations number (call (800) 555-1212 to get it) which is serviced even during non-business hours.

However, if you don't know exactly what you want, airline ticket agents have neither the information nor the training to suggest a wide range of options. It is not part of their job—as it is a travel agent's—to be familiar with particular hotels and attractions at your destination.

Second, your options will be limited to hotels and car rentals available through that particular airline's computer. Third, while a travel agent will be able to provide you with a written confirmation of your hotel or car reservation, airline ticket agents do not.

Although all of your reservations should be in the computer, it can be frustrating to deal with the airlines because you never speak to the same person twice. Every time you call, you reach a different, anonymous agent to whom you must explain your needs from scratch.

Booking by Personal Computer

Technology has brought us a third method of booking hotels and airlines—using a computer in the privacy and comfort of home or office. Check with the various services listed below for details, but generally all you need is an IBM-compatible home computer with communications capabilities and a certain minimum of capacity.

The simplest, most straightforward service comes through

the OAG (Official Airline Guides) Electronic Edition, which can flash up on your screen the same flight and fare information available to your travel or airlines agent. One benefit of using this system is that you can personally search for the most advantageous fare, and don't need to rely on a perhaps harried or non-motivated third person to find it for you. OAG says that the fare and schedule information for North America is updated daily, and for international flights, weekly. You can actually reserve your seat by following a series of commands which appear on the computer screen. Once it's reserved, you can have your tickets written and sent to you by Thomas Cook Travel USA or arrange to pick them up at the airport. This system may not be used to buy tickets through other travel agencies.

The one-time sign-up fee for the OAG service also gives you access to hotel and motel information in North America, Europe and the Pacific. Beyond the sign-up fee, there are no charges for a session which results in a booking, review or cancellation of reservations.

For sessions which don't result in a transaction, charges are incurred for each minute. In addition, you are charged for the number of screens of information you use.

If you belong to computer information services such as The Source or Compuserve, you can use the OAG Electronic Edition through them. Each also provides access to additional travel information. But because the primary purpose of these services is not travel information, you'll be paying a sign-up fee, a monthly fee and fees for the time you're using the system. See the appendix for information on how to contact these services.

Telephone Booking

Booking through (800) numbers: Virtually all major hotel and car rental chains now offer reservations through toll-free telephone numbers. If you're an experienced traveler who knows exactly what you want this can be a fast way to make your arrangements. If you're choosy about your hotel room or the services available, you can often get detailed information about the accommodations and facilities through these reservation services.

If you've chosen to book a hotel by yourself, be sure to ask for all of the room rates. Often a "corporate" rate is available simply for the asking. In many cases hotels offer a package which the reservations service doesn't bother to mention unless you ask about it. In addition, rates vary tremendously according to season.

Sometimes you can even negotiate an advantageous rate if the hotelier knows that occupancy will be lagging on the date you're seeking. But you're more likely to be successful doing this if you call the hotel directly, rather than the toll-free number for the chain or reservations service.

If you want to reserve a package tour offered by an airline, you may need to be referred to the "tour desk," which generally only answers the phone during normal working hours.

Before You Book

It is YOUR trip, and no matter how much help is available you'll have to do some of the preparation.

If the goal is something more complicated than the annual flight to visit Mom and Dad, or the monthly business trip to a branch office, invest a little time in research.

If you're bargain-hunting, read the newspaper ads. Neither a travel agent nor an airlines agent can keep up with the constant changes. If you can say: "I think there's a $178 round trip flight from Washington to California," they know how to check it out for you. The same advice goes for business travelers seeking the most economical, comfortable business or first-class service. Often the best way to find out which airline offers a "sleeper" seat for the trip to Tokyo is to take note of the ads in the business publications you read.

Do likewise with tour packages for popular routes. If you're considering a summer trip to England, start watching the ads and the travel advice columns in your local paper to spot the best fare or package, and to get ideas about itineraries. (See Chapter Ten, "Your Rights as a Travel Consumer," for tips on how to make sure you're dealing with a reputable tour operator.) If you're destination-hunting for your next vacation, check some guidebooks out of the library or pick one up in the bookstore. Ask your friends for suggestions. You'll get much better service if you don't start your conversation with a travel agent by saying, "Where can I go that's warm in January?"

Booking Tips

To locate toll-free numbers, dial information at (800) 555-1212.

If you can, plan ahead. As obvious as this sounds, many people don't realize how many more hotels, fares and destinations they will have to choose from if they do their research. Planning will also generally increase the availability of bargain airfares.

But do not reserve before you're sure where and when you want to go. Many airlines, hotels and tour packagers charge a penalty for a cancellation or for changing a date of arrival, departure or reservation.

Always ask what the penalties are—before you buy. In order to get a bargain round trip, advance purchase fare from New York to Bombay, it might be worth it to incur a $75 penalty in the event that you may need to change the date of return. But the "cheaper" fare certainly won't be worth it if you have to buy a whole new ticket in order to return on a different date.

When booking flights, always request a seat assignment and, if possible, get your boarding pass with the ticket. This can reduce the time you spend waiting in airport lines.

It may also reduce your risk of ending up scrunched into a middle seat or in a section which does not meet your smoking or non-smoking choice. U.S. carriers are required to ban smoking on all domestic flights of less than two hours. But for longer or international flights you'll still need to request a seat in the smoking or non-smoking section.

When booking a flight, order a special meal if appropriate. Airlines offer a much wider range of special meals than is generally known. In addition to those which meet religious or medical requirements—such as vegetarian or "American Traveler" menus developed by American Airlines with the American Heart Association—many airlines will offer alternatives such as a seafood or fruit salad, or

TWA's "Kansas City Barbecue Platter," complete with corn pudding and black-eyed peas. You or your travel agent can ask the airline what options are available. Most airlines require that the request for a special meal be made 24 hours before departure.

If you're going on a tour or signing up for a package, ask your travel agent about insurance against cancellation and delays.

Use off-peak hours to make airlines, car rental or hotel chain reservations. If time is of the essence, you can usually get through to the airlines on the phone faster at 7:30 p.m. or even at midnight than during the normal business hours.

Sometimes you can win big in a last-minute game of booking roulette. Blocks of hotel rooms or airplane seats are sometimes reserved and then released closer to the effective date. In the case of airplanes, you may also benefit at the last minute from the constant, unpredictable changes in fare structure. Some organizations which advertise in travel publications offer last-minute "bargains" to a range of destinations. Before booking through these types of agencies, be sure to check them out with your local Better Business Bureau or other consumer protection agency.

When booking flights, be aware of the difference between "direct," which means you won't have to change aircraft, but the plane may make other stops; and "non-stop," which means just that. For example, if your direct flight from coast to coast is scheduled to stop in a busy hub airport such as Chicago or Atlanta, the risk of delays is greater than on a non-stop.

TRAVELER'S CHECKLIST
BOOKINGS

••••••••••••••••••••••••••••••••••

☐ **1.** Check transportation tickets for accuracy.

☐ **2.** Confirm flights.

☐ **3.** Check all vouchers for accuracy.

☐ **4.** Leave copy of tickets and vouchers at home; give another to traveling companion.

☐ **5.** Bring along copy of airline and train schedules.

☐ **6.** Bring along travel agent's phone number to use in emergency.

_____

_____

_____

_____

_____

_____

_____

_____

_____

_____

_____

Chapter Two

COPING WITH OFFICIALDOM

A routine three-day business trip to London may require nothing but a current passport. But a two-month, open-ended journey around South America or Africa warrants addressing the formalities a few months ahead of time.

Crossing an international border—whether to enter a foreign country or return to your own—can be one of the most memorable aspects of a journey. But although the memories may be vivid, they are not always good.

Americans tend to be welcome in most parts of the world, but getting yourself and your possessions into another country and back to your own can be very frustrating if you're not aware of the pitfalls and the rules beforehand.

Border-crossing experiences can also vary depending on where you're arriving and who your traveling companions are. Cases in point were my entries into London with a planeload of Indians arriving from New Delhi; and into Málaga, Spain where most of my companions on the flight were Arabs coming from Morocco. In both cases—probably due to concerns about terrorism, drug smuggling, and illegal immigration—border formalities proceeded much more slowly and thoroughly than had been my experience arriving in those countries on flights from the U.S. or from Europe, where most of my fellow passengers were Americans or Europeans.

As an international traveler, you have two commodities

---

to worry about—your person and your possessions.

A passport, visas, and health documents are the tickets to successful international transfer of the person. But the more things you bring along or want to take home—luggage, money, a personal computer, food—the more potential complications arise and the more forethought is required.

To smooth the crossing as much as possible, you should learn before departure about the rules and regulations to be encountered, and be prepared both to produce the necessary documents and to avoid situations which could delay or prevent crossing.

The State Department estimates that 20 to 25 million Americans hold current passports. The number of us who use them depends on many factors, including the value of the dollar overseas, concerns about international terrorism and the state of our economy at home. But regardless of how often we travel internationally, what needs to be done to comply with legal formalities breaks down into three phases—before you go, while you're on the road, and when you come home.

"Know before you go" is particularly apt advice when it comes to crossing borders. The immigration or customs office—whether it's in a modern airport or in a shack at a border in the jungle—is the last place you place you want to spend either your vacation or your business time.

Before You Go

Here's a run-down of what to do before you leave. The more complicated, extensive or uncertain your trip, the further ahead you should plan.

Passport: Details of how and where to secure a U.S. passport can be found in "Your Trip Abroad," a State Department publication. (See box.) Details are not enumerated here because requirements and procedures change occasionally. So before you march to the local passport office, inform yourself about costs, required documents (you'll definitely need either your old passport or other proof of U.S. citizenship such as a birth certificate), pictures and other requirements for the application.

You can apply for a passport by mail or in person. There are 13 U.S. passport agencies, located for the most part in major cities. If you live in a city which does not have an agency, or in a rural or isolated area, your main post office or local clerk of the court may be able to process your application or guide you to another agency which can do it.

Be sure to read the fine print in the requirements about documents and bring along (or mail) everything you'll need, to avoid extra hassles. Even seasoned international travelers should note a relatively new requirement: when you apply for a new passport, you'll be requested to provide your Social Security number. (This will be used to help the Internal Revenue Service track down American residents overseas who may be shirking their tax obligations.)

According to the State Department, the heavy demand for passports starts each year in January and continues through June. Thus it's recommended that you apply between July and the end of the year to get speedier service. In the high season, it can take several weeks to receive a passport, even if it's a renewal. However, State Department officials say that they always try to respond quickly to travelers who need to depart suddenly because of an emergency.

Visas: A visa is a permit to enter and travel in a foreign country which is entered into your passport in the form of a stamp. Most countries outside of Europe and Canada and Mexico require U.S. citizens to have a visa to enter and spend a certain amount of time. (Because of concern about terrorism, France is an exception in Western Europe—tourists must now have a visa to visit there.)

Visa requirements and the amount of time you'll be allowed to remain there may depend on both the status of its relationship to the U.S. and the purpose of your trip. Most countries which require tourists to have visas routinely allow them to stay a few weeks or months. However, if you're going on business, you may be asked to provide information about your business intentions or contacts. And in some cases, a visa alone will not get you into the country. When you request visa information, be sure you ask about ALL the requirements for entering and staying in a particular country.

Burma, for example, requires visitors to have a visa for the next destination or an onward or return ticket. Cameroon requires tourists to present a bank statement. Visitors to El Salvador must show that they have $300 in their possession in order to enter the country.

If you plan to visit several countries on one journey, learn about visa and other requirements several months ahead of time, if possible. Embassies—which represent foreign governments to the U.S. government—tend to be in Washington, DC. But many countries also have consulates which issue visas, facilitate foreign trade and sometimes offer other services or information to Americans interested in their country, in other parts of the U.S. In a major city, check the local phone book. If you don't live near the embassy or consulates of the countries you'll be visiting, you'll need to apply by mail. Often a travel agent can save you time and trouble by making applications for you.

However, if you're on your own, check guidebooks or the *Congressional Directory* (available in most libraries) for a list of embassies in the U.S.; or order the State Department's pamphlet, "Foreign Consular Offices in the United States."

Once you've located the embassy or consulate, the first step is to find out what information you must submit to get a visa, because it can vary drastically. You will be required to submit your passport and in most cases, you'll need to submit one or more photographs. In some cases you'll be charged a visa fee. Some countries even require proof that you have purchased a ticket to leave the country before they will let you in.

For a trip to several countries which require visas, getting all of this together can take weeks or months. There is really no way to shortcut the process. Even though you might choose to do this by express mail, no one can make a consulate give you a visa faster than they want to. You—or your travel agent—simply must fill out the forms, send your application to one consulate or embassy; wait for the passport with visa to be returned; and then do the same thing all over again for each country you intend to visit. Your passport, unfortunately, can only be in one place at one time.

If you're likely to travel in and out of a country several

times during your visit, be sure to request a multiple entry visa so that you don't have to reapply each time.

One more cautionary note: when you receive the visas, recheck them to make sure the dates are correct. Human error is possible, and you don't want to discover it when you arrive at your foreign destination.

If all of the above sounds like a frustrating hassle, just keep in mind that the preparation is a minor irritation compared to the difficulties you could face arriving at the border of a country for which you do NOT have a visa. The State Department's list of visa requirements notes that, in the case of several countries, visitors arriving at an airport without a visa could be subject to significant delays.

Driver's License: If you plan to drive overseas, ask about the license requirements at the same time you request visa information. The American Automobile Association can also tell you whether it's advisable or necessary to have an international driver's license to drive in certain countries. These can be easily obtained through AAA. Check your own license to make sure it will not expire while you're away from home.

Political Climate: If you have any doubts about the safety or the political climate of the country you're visiting, request information from the U.S. State Department's Citizen's Emergency Center. The telephone number is (202) 647-5225. The Center will inform you of the existence of any special travel warnings or advice which may be in effect. The State Department also publishes booklets about specific currency, visa, health and even cultural problems you might encounter encounter if you travel to certain destinations— Cuba, Saudi Arabia and others—which are known to be risky or sensitive for American visitors. (See "Tips for Travelers" series cited in box.)

Customs Requirements—Destination Country: The international traveler must contend with two sets of customs requirements and procedures—those of the country or countries visited, and those of the U.S. When you contact a foreign embassy or consulate about getting a visa, ask for information about customs requirements. Don't forget that you're subject to customs checks both on the way into a country and on the way out. For example, the souvenir you bought in Thailand has to be acceptable to the customs officials in Singapore if that's the next stop on your itinerary.

U.S. GOVERNMENT INFORMATION FOR TRAVELERS

Federal agencies publish useful information for Americans traveling abroad, ranging from warnings about the red tape and conditions they are likely to encounter in foreign lands (and advice on how to deal with them) to the U.S. government rules and restrictions that will greet them upon their return home. All of the publications can be purchased for nominal fees from the Superintendent of Documents, U.S. Government Printing Office, Washington, DC 20402. (See Appendix A, General Resources, for information on how to order and pay for publications from the GPO.) Some of the best:

■ "Your Trip Abroad," Department of State Publication 8872, contains such information as how to obtain a passport, visas, and what if any immunizations are required for your trip.

■ "Foreign Visa Requirements," Department of State Publication 9517, provides a country-by-country list of visa requirements and phone numbers of foreign embassies from which you can get more information and applications.

■ "Know Before You Go: Customs Hints for Returning Residents," Treasury Department Publication No. 512, describes customs laws in considerable detail and contains charts which explain how much

But the souvenirs may be the least of your problems. Almost all countries place a limit on the quantity of cigarettes and alcohol you can bring in, and restrictions on agricultural products, foodstuffs and foreign currency are also common. Saudi Arabia prohibits the entry of alcohol in any form including, according to the State Department, an in-

duty is assessed on various items you may want to bring into the U.S.

■ "Customs Hints for Visitors (Nonresidents)," Treasury Department Publication No. 511, explains the regulations that apply to non-residents entering the U.S. It would be helpful, for example, if foreign relatives wanted to bring you large or unusual presents during a visit to the United States.

■ "Travelers' Tips on Bringing Food, Plant, and Animal Products into the United States," Department of Agriculture Program Aid No. 1083, explains what you can and cannot return with from your overseas trip. It includes a list of permissible products as well as instructions on how to enter the U.S. with an animal.

■ "Tips for Travelers to . . ." is a series of State Department publications that advises travelers about safety, legal, cultural and other special concerns before visiting particular sensitive areas.

■ "Travel Warning on Drugs Abroad," a State Department brochure, tells the hard facts about the legal status and likely treatment of American citizens arrested overseas on drug charges. It also provides information on how to help a fellow American who may be detained.

ebriated traveler who's overdone it on the flight into the country.

Religious, political, health, conservation and other considerations can result in restrictions on a wide range of products. Arriving in a Communist country in Eastern Europe, I watched customs officials confiscate *Time* magazine and every other western newspaper and magazine they encountered in the visitors' luggage.

Antiques, art or cultural treasures, a stuffed version of the game you bagged on safari, ivory, gemstones or a leopard-skin coat may all be prohibited exports. Items made of sea-turtle, crocodile and animal furs are all likely to be refused entry to the U.S. because they are endangered species. Some countries are particularly strict on visitors who try to take home archaeological or cultural relics. One American traveler learned about these sensitivities the hard way when she was imprisoned in Turkey, charged with trying to smuggle out of the country a carved wooden head which the authorities claimed was a Roman antique.

Customs Requirements—Returning to the U.S.: I'll never forget the look of distress on the faces of two grandmotherly ladies arriving at New York's JFK Airport from their Caribbean island home when the customs agent shook his head, clicked his tongue and confiscated from them two enormous plastic bags bulging with fresh, obviously very spicy, peppers.

Food—especially items which are raw or unprocessed— is only one of many types of items which are subject to special requirements or prohibitions. Anything which is or was recently alive (from a pet to a stuffed gamefish caught in the Pacific Ocean to the tropical plant you couldn't resist buying in the local market) is likely to be covered by Department of Agriculture regulations.

Items made of sea-turtle, crocodile, and animal furs are all likely to be refused entry to the U.S. because they are endangered species. Large amounts of money, luxury goods such as jewelry and furs, firearms and drugs can all cause you problems at a time when all you want to do is get home and get some sleep.

"Know Before You Go" is the theme trumpeted by the U.S.

How to Plan a Successful Trip

Customs Service (and the name of the pamphlet which outlines the rules). Following the advice in the pamphlet can smooth your re-entry to the U.S. In general, returning citizens may bring in $400 worth of goods before they have to start paying duty. However, the rules are complicated and depend on factors such as where you are coming from. So get the book, read it and even consider packing it in your suitcase for last-minute reference before your return. For rules on plants and animals and their products, check the USDA pamphlet listed in the accompanying box.

Some unlucky travelers may end up paying duty on items they had bought in the U.S. and taken along on an overseas trip. Even if you bought it in the U.S., any foreign-made article in your possession when you return—a portable computer, camera equipment, expensive watch, etc.—is po-

---

AMERICANS ARRESTED ABROAD: FOR WHAT AND WHERE

In 1986, more than 2,800 Americans were arrested in 101 foreign countries, nearly a third of them for drug possession.

After possession of illegal drugs, the other most common reasons for arrest of Americans overseas are immigration violations, which accounted for 12 percent in 1986; followed by fraud, theft, drunk or disorderly conduct and possession of a deadly weapon.

The largest number of arrests occurred in Mexico (681), Jamaica (272), Canada (259), the Bahamas (212), the Federal Republic of Germany (183), and the Dominican Republic (133). The State Department says that these six countries consistently account for the most arrest cases—in 1986, for 62% of all arrests of Americans worldwide.

The countries with the largest numbers of the total of 1388 Americans in custody at the end of the same year were Mexico, Canada, Federal Republic of Germany and the United Kingdom, in that order.

---

tentially dutiable if you haven't registered it with the U.S. Customs Service before departure.

It is impossible to register these articles by mail. You must personally take the article to a U.S. Customs office, where you'll be asked to fill in a form which requires the serial number of the item. Customs authorities will then give you the form to carry with your passport. On your return to the U.S., show the form and you'll avoid paying duty. If there's no Customs Office handy, you can always find one at an international airport. However, always call ahead to find out the location and the office hours so you can allow time to go there without missing your flight.

In order to avoid both duties and hassles with customs officials both in the U.S. and overseas, business travelers can secure a document known as a "carnet" from the United States Council for International Business, 1212 Avenue of the Americas, New York, NY 10036. Phone is (212) 354-4480.

With the vouchers provided, you can travel with—or send ahead—not only items such as a personal computer for your own use, but also tools and goods you may need to conduct business, participate in trade shows, or give product demonstrations. Among the goods covered are office equipment, surgical and dental equipment, jewelry and precious stones, agricultural machinery, furniture, and much more. The carnet is accepted by more than 40 countries and territories including Europe and many in Asia and the Pacific.

When You Get There/On The Road

Border Crossings: The experience of crossing a border can be anything from fast and perfunctory to slow, laborious and frustrating—or even dangerous. But with your passport, visa and other requirements anticipated and provided for, you have the best chance of entering a foreign country with a minimum of problems. Regardless of the frustration or delay which might arise, try to keep a cool head and if asked questions, respond politely and fully.

The treatment you receive from customs officials may depend as much on where you've been as on who you are.

How to Plan a Successful Trip

If you're coming from Bolivia or Colombia, known for their drug trade, or Burma, known for its black market in gemstones, you may be questioned and your luggage may be examined more thoroughly than you'd otherwise expect.

Passport Preservation: Keep your passport with you, concealed as much as possible, and be sure to have the number written down elsewhere in your luggage as well as at home. (Some travelers carry a photocopy of the first few pages of the passport in a separate part of their luggage or give it to their traveling companion. This can speed re-issue if you should find yourself without a passport in a foreign country.)

If you're roaming the desert in a Middle Eastern country or the jungle in South America, keep your passport with you all the time. In Morocco, for example, I found that even on short excursions by car outside of Marrakech I was asked repeatedly to show my passport at checkpoints. In some countries you may be asked to produce the passport before you're allowed to check into a hotel. (Some countries actually require the hotel to keep your passport while you're registered.) Some hotel personnel don't want to do the paperwork on the spot and request you to "leave your passport here for a while" at the reception desk. In these cases, insist that you will wait while they fill out the forms. Try to avoid ever having your passport left at the reception desk or sitting in a mailbox which is accessible and visible to anyone who walks by the counter.

However, if you're in a reliable hotel—especially in a big city—it's often safer to leave the passport locked in a safe deposit box than to carry it in your pocket or purse into the crowds.

Registering With the Embassy: The U.S. has 250 Foreign Service posts and an additional 35 consular offices throughout the world. The State Department suggests that you register and leave a copy of your itinerary with the U.S. embassy if you plan to be in the country longer than a month, are visiting Eastern European Communist countries or plan to visit a country where there may be civil unrest or political disturbances. If you are visiting countries where there is no U.S. representation such as Albania or South Yemen, register with the U.S. embassy or consulate in a neighboring country.

Customs Reminder: If you expect to make many or valuable purchases, keep records which will protect you against unpleasant surprises when you return to the U.S. or enter another country. Keep receipts for your purchases.

American citizens generally are entitled to bring in (personally, not by mail) $400 worth of purchases duty-free. The next $1,000 worth of purchases—as long as they are for your use or are gifts—will be assessed duty of 10 percent of the fair retail value. Purchases you mail to the U.S.—unless they are gifts worth less than $50 each—will be analyzed and subjected to duty on arrival. These are not included in the $400 exemption.

There are details and exceptions to the above rules, some based on the length of time you've been away, some based on where you did your shopping and what you bought. Before you buy, make sure you know what the customs consequences will be. "Know Before You Go," the Customs Service pamphlet, is the best source of information. However, it's worth correcting here some of the most common misunderstandings about what will generate duty:

1. Clothes and other items you bought and used or wore overseas must be declared.

2. Items purchased in "duty free shops" abroad are subject to U.S. customs regulations.

3. Duty cannot be avoided by sending small purchases home and labeling them as gifts. You are entitled to send individual packages, each worth no more than $50, as gifts. You may not send them to yourself or to your traveling companions, and you can only send one a day to a particular person.

Legal Problems: The most serious legal problem which can prevent you from returning home is landing in jail. In 1986, more than 2,800 Americans were arrested in 101 foreign countries, nearly a third of them for drug possession—in many cases, for possessing one ounce or less of the substance.

The State Department offers this strong advice to travelers tempted to engage in illegal activities:

- Presence in a foreign country makes you subject to its laws, even if you are a U.S. citizen.

- Ignorance of the law does not absolve you of guilt.

- U.S. consular officials can visit you in jail, notify friends and family and try to help you in other ways. But they cannot get you out of jail.

- Criminal justice procedures in foreign countries can be lengthy and costly, prison conditions may be very primitive, and penalties are often stiffer than in the U.S.

Coming Home

Emergencies: U.S. consular authorities are the ones to contact for advice and assistance about emergencies which require you to return home suddenly, or which impede your ability to return.

Marine guards posted at U.S. embassies 24 hours a day can put you in touch with a duty officer if you or a traveling companion faces a life or death emergency. If you come to them during non-business hours with a problem of less severity, they will probably ask you to wait until normal working hours.

If you or a traveling companion becomes seriously ill or dies, or if you are robbed of your passport and money, contact the closest U.S. Embassy or consulate for help. If necessary, they can help you identify the proper local authorities—a process which might be difficult and frustrating for a short-term visitor.

Passport: When returning to the U.S. you'll be asked to show your passport and to tell immigration officials where you have traveled and for what purpose. These are routine questions and shouldn't cause any concern.

Customs Preparations: Before going through U.S. customs you'll be required to fill out a declaration form to report on how much money you spent on purchases outside the U.S. A customs inspector may choose to open and search your luggage. Try to streamline your encounter with U.S. Customs by having luggage keys and receipts handy and packing articles you bought near the top of your luggage.

Paying Duty: After checking your documents and perhaps your luggage, the Customs officer will return your declaration form and tell you if it is necessary to pay duty on your purchases.

Assessments on items not subject to flat rates are based on the nature of the article and where it was purchased. In general, rates are higher on goods bought or made in Communist countries. Tariffs on particular items might range from, for example, 3.8 percent on a camera to 5 percent on chocolate candy to 27.5 percent on jewelry made of precious metals.

You'll have to pay duty before you leave the Customs area. At most major airports you may now pay with a credit card. Call your nearest U.S. Customs Service office to ascertain which cards are accepted and at which airports. Other acceptable methods of payment are U.S. currency (not foreign currency); a personal check; and a government or traveler's check (not worth more than $50 over your bill) or a money order.

Customs officials have the right to impose penalties as well as duty if you fail to declare an article or if you present a bill which shows a false or understated value. For the casual traveler who has inadvertently forgotten to declare a purchase or who has under-declared, and who has no previous record of customs violations, the penalty is likely to be financial—e.g., equal to the value of the purchase.

Criminal penalties—including jail—can be imposed on travelers who are proven to have broken the law intentionally, to have brought in large quantities of under-declared or undeclared goods (especially for commercial purposes), and who have a record of previous violations.

TRAVELER'S CHECKLIST
OFFICIALDOM
••••••••••••••••••••••••••••••••••

- [ ] **1.** Make sure passport is current; renew if necessary.

- [ ] **2.** Secure visas.

- [ ] **3.** Bring along photocopy of first few pages of passport.

- [ ] **4.** Pack extra passport photos.

- [ ] **5.** Bring along U.S. or international driver's license.

- [ ] **6.** Bring along address and phone numbers of U.S. embassies and consulates.

- [ ] **7.** Contact State Department for update if visiting a trouble spot.

- [ ] **8.** Study customs regulations for destinations and return to U.S.

_____

_____

_____

_____

_____

_____

_____

_____

Chapter Three

HOW TO CHOOSE A HOTEL

All travelers, regardless of their destination or mission, look for the perfect hotel. Perfection, of course, is defined by individual needs and tastes. Opinions on the subject diverge quickly into two major schools of thought. One school views the hotel as a necessary evil, "just a place to sleep," and argues that "I won't spend any time there anyway." Adherents of the second school don't just think of the hotel as important, but see it as the ultimate destination, the raison d'être of the journey which must offer at least the comforts of home but preferably all of those and many more.

Believers in the "necessary evil" philosophy are more likely to find themselves in a fourth-floor bathless walk-up on the Left Bank in Paris than in the Ritz. But they may also choose to stay in a $150 or $200 per night room in a sterile but supremely practical high-rise "businessman's hotel" on the basis of access to a telex machine and the airport rather than charm.

In my early days of traveling, the cost of the room was the most important factor in choosing a hotel. After inquiring about rates, I and my youthful companions often walked out of one hotel to another down the street for the sake of saving one dollar a night. We also covered a lot of ground, shifting from one hotel to another in a nearby town or from one major city to another.

With the passage of time and an increase in travel for business rather than pleasure, however, my standards for a minimum of comfort became higher.

Thus I slid slowly but surely into that second school of wanderers who try to change hotels as little as possible and who take the trouble to seek out a comfortable, even alluring environment even if they'll only be there for a few nights.

Years of journeys have fed my fantasies about and requirements for the "dream hotel." Sometimes the dreams have been nightmares which have brought into sharper focus the requirements of the ideal hotel.

Ambiance and Service

I learned that regardless of where a hotel is located, ambiance and service are important ingredients which can make or break your stay.

A particularly unfortunate ambiance tempted me and my companions to flee from a cavernous concrete cell where three cots reposed at rakish angles and lizards scampered across the floor at a hostelry in northern India many years ago.

A more pleasurable ambiance made my blood pressure level decline and whisked away thoughts of home the next night when I was rocked gently to sleep in an elegantly appointed houseboat on a lily-padded lake in the shadow of the Himalayas.

Thoughtful, friendly service helped to heal my altitude sickness and chills when it came in the form of a roaring fire and a hot cup of coca de mate (the local remedy) tea in the hotel lounge at more than 10,000 feet in Cuzco, Peru.

But lack of understanding of the concept of service is what kept my traveling companion awake until 2 a.m. arguing with a clerk in an empty hotel lobby in Rome who "didn't have time" to place a call to the U.S.

Define Your Needs

Dissecting the characteristics of a dream hotel and putting them together again could result in a hostelry which no architect could construct—and no traveler will ever encounter.

But for any traveler who spends more than an occasional night in a hotel, it's generally worth investing some time before departure to find a hotel which will contribute to making the trip successful. The process of finding such a hotel is pretty much the same regardless of the purpose of the trip.

Think for a minute:

How long is this trip? Can you stay in one hotel the entire time or must you change hotels often? The pension or airport hotel where you'll sleep for seven hours but barely unpack your suitcase before catching the next train or plane does not have to offer the most sophisticated eating, laundry, or communications facilities. But your "home away from home" for a week of intense business negotiations should be a place where you will receive your telephone messages, where the kitchen never closes, the laundry is done fast and well, and, if it's your thing—there's a swimming pool, health club or jogging track to help relieve the tension.

What will you be doing all day? The business traveler may spend little time in a hotel but require certain services when he or she is there—or even when he's not. The vacationer on the "grand tour" may intend to spend the whole day sightseeing and may prefer to avoid telephones, crowds in the lobby and the higher rates which must be paid once the facilities and services go beyond a clean, comfortable bed and coffee and croissants in the morning. The vacationer who travels in luxury may consider a large, well-equipped room with sofa, mini-bar and video player necessary trappings. Sort it out before you make a reservation. To help you determine what you will need we've provided an accompanying box containing a checklist of hotel features.

How to Get the Best Rates

Take advantage of your membership in a frequent flyer or other type of frequent traveler club (some of which are now sponsored by hotels) to secure special rates, facilities or services in certain hotels. Other types of memberships— for example, in a travel club, the American Automobile Association or the American Association for Retired Persons— may also entitle you to discount rates.

Hotel rates change with the seasons. If you have some flexibility, it may be worth scheduling your trip a week earlier or postponing it slightly to take advantage of the off-season. You or your travel agent can find out the rates by asking the hotel or reservations service. Do not assume that all hotels or resort areas change their rates on exactly the same dates. Definition of the season depends heavily on where you're going. In Spain, the tourist season—with higher rates—runs from about June to October but also includes the Christmas holidays and Easter. In Australia, prices go down around April for their fall and winter season. In recent years many European hotels have been offering bargains to attract Americans to visit during the winter.

Also, especially in the U.S., some of the best big-city hotels—which are filled with business travelers during the week—offer the same rooms for half the price on the weekend.

If you are traveling alone, you are likely to find that you are charged the rate for a double room. As more modern hotel rooms are designed to accommodate at least two people, this has become commonplace. If you want to vacation alone and don't want to pay these rates, about the only option you have is to work with a tour organization such as Singleworld [(800) 223-6490] that specializes in serving single travelers and will try to match roommates to share hotel rooms, cruise cabins, etc. Another tour company that has a lot of single clients and says it will find an appropriate roommate for you is Cosmos Tours [(800) 556-5454].

Finally, be sure to ask a prospective hotel whether it has reduced rates either for senior citizens, family groups or business travelers. (In the last case, the magic phrase is "corporate rate.") Reporters for one travel magazine found that when they insisted, they could pry more favorable rates out of reservations clerks by insisting that they check the computer for special packages, or for the rates above and below the first one quoted.

How to Locate the Right Hotel

The first step in choosing a hotel is to decide on the appropriate geographic location. Defining the area where you seek a hotel can be relatively simple if your mission is business and "everything" happens downtown. If you're vacationing, more options will be available.

But regardless of where and why you're traveling, consider the relationship of your hotel's location to your transportation needs. If your dream is to visit the Vatican and the Spanish Steps in Rome, should you stay in the outskirts? Are buses, taxis or commuter trains fast and accessible?

Center city locations offer convenience to shops, restaurants and cultural attractions. Moreover, these are the accommodations best known to travel agents.

However, your hotel dollar will generally buy less in a central location in a big city. Thus if your budget is tight, the accommodations from which you can choose may be less comfortable and attractive than they would be in another neighborhood.

If you'll be going out at night and returning to the hotel late, it's important to feel comfortable in the neighborhood—unless you can afford door-to-door taxi service every time. Unsafe neighborhoods where pickpockets and other undesirables may lurk are more likely to be found in the center of the city than in more residential areas or in small towns.

Finally, a well-built, well-insulated modern hotel may shut out most street noise—perhaps to a fault. But if you're not used to the clang of garbage cans in the middle of the night or the revving up of motorcycles at morning rush hour or the cacophony of revelers leaving the bars at closing time, beware of taking a room in a small hotel or pension on a major traffic artery or in a neighborhood with a lot of nightlife. Before you check in, take a look at how the hotel is situated. In some cases it's worth sacrificing "the view" over a busy street for the relative quiet of a room in the back of the hotel.

For a more relaxed, non-business trip which allows you to meander through countryside and small towns, don't assume it's necessary to sleep in a different hotel every night. Do yourself a favor by spending several nights in one charming, comfortable spot and making daily excursions to other towns, the beach, or the mountains. You'll avoid some of the inevitable wear and tear of packing up and

SELECTING A HOTEL—A CHECKLIST

For your trip, what facilities and services do you require to be comfortable and happy? Here's a checklist to consider before choosing a hotel. You can ask your travel agent or reservations agent to help you find the answers before you make your selection:

■ Is there air conditioning and/or heat? In the U.S. this is unlikely to be an issue but a low-budget hotel in the tropics may lack air conditioning, and a pension in a European city may provide a space heater, but nothing that most Americans would classify as "heat."

■ What business services are available? (See Chapter Eight, "Accommodating the Business Traveler.")

■ Are cribs, cots, and other special furnishings or room configurations for children available? (See Chapter Nine, "When A Family Travels.")

■ How about child care? (See Chapter Nine, "When A Family Travels.")

■ Cleaning: Is it important to have the room put in order more than once a day?

■ Elevators: If you or someone in your party has difficulty climbing stairs is there an alternative?

■ Are there available financial services such as currency exchange, check cashing, payment of bills by credit card or travelers check?

■ Laundry: Can it be done by the hotel or is there access to a washing machine, dryer and iron?

■ Small luxuries: A fresh terry cloth bathrobe every day; flowers on the desk; complimentary shampoo, razor, toiletries; a mint on the pillow. Are these important to you?

■ Are non-smoking rooms or floors available? In the U.S. and in hotels affiliated with major world-wide chains, such as Hilton and Inter-Continental, it is increasingly possible to request and acquire these.

■ What is available in the way of recreation and sports—health club, swimming pool, jogging track, golf course—either in the hotel or nearby?

■ Does the hotel contain restaurants, bars and facilities for entertaining? Open all night or almost all night?

■ Room service: Food and drink available 24 hours a day or less?

■ Do security measures include safe deposit boxes in the lobby or in the room, numberless keys which can't be identified if you lose them, 24-hour desk service? If you stay in a small, "charming" inn or pension—in the U.S. or overseas—you may not receive any of these features.

■ Can you buy in the hotel such items as newspapers and toothpaste?

■ Is there a telephone in the room?

■ Women's services: Some hotels pride themselves on providing hair dryers, make-up kits and extra security measures for women. One hotel chain even offers to arrange for businesswomen traveling alone to share a dining room table with other solo travelers. Are any of these services important to you?

moving each morning and worrying about whether you'll find an appropriate hotel that night.

Best of all, you'll feel more a part of the area you're visiting. If you stay a few days in the same hotel, local shopkeepers and waiters will start to recognize and greet you, and you'll experience the daily rhythm of the place in a way that you never could as a tourist who is constantly on the move.

This happened to me in Bali, Indonesia, where a local resident invited me and my traveling companion to the dedication of a new house. We spent several unforgettable hours, wandering through the torch-illuminated yard, watching shadow puppet performances and graceful Balinese dancers and listening to the harmonious plunking of two gamelan orchestras assembled for the occasion.

How to Check Out a Hotel

There's no substitute for the advice of a trusted friend or travel agent who has stayed in the hotel recently.

Price can be but is not always a good measure of the quality of a hotel. If you can afford to stay at the most expensive lodgings in town, they will probably offer a certain minimum of comfort—but not necessarily value.

This chapter describes how to identify hotels through (800) numbers and airline reservations systems, but especially for vacationers who seek unusual, out-of-the-way or low-budget accommodations, this system has its limitations. What else can you do?

When seeking the recommendations of your traveling the recommendations of your traveling friends and colleagues, make sure that you seek advice from people whose standards and interests are similar to yours. If you start far enough ahead of your journey, chances are you'll find someone who's been to the same destination fairly recently.

Read guidebooks and compare their recommendations. Guidebooks can help you identify hotels, but not all of them provide equally thorough or up to date information. If you're going to buy a guidebook, study the format carefully. Does the book actually list facilities and services available in each hotel (e.g., bar, restaurant, parking, swimming pool, etc.), or does it simply describe the lodgings in general terms ("modest," "well-located," "typical," etc.)? It's often more useful to have an explicit list of facilities than to depend on a general recommendation or rating by a writer you don't know.

If you can't tell from the book, ask your bookseller to check for you how recently the volume has been updated. Not all guidebooks are updated every year. I once updated a guidebook chapter on a South American city three years after it had been written. Nearly half the hotels in the earlier edition no longer existed, yet the book was still being sold.

Prices especially go out of date fast. If cost is an important issue for you and you're going overseas, inform yourself about what's happened to the dollar and to prices in that country since the book was written. In the course of one year Spain joined the European Community and imposed a value added tax on most transactions and the American dollar declined precipitously. Suddenly the rate for a room in my favorite hotels in Madrid and Barcelona changed from a bargain to virtually beyond my means.

Compare hotel listings and recommendations. Do two or three books agree on which are the best hotels in a price category or location? Do they even mention the same hotels?

Public tourist authorities are frequently good sources of information. Virtually every state and many cities in the U.S. publish lists of accommodations. In other countries it is common to publish not just a hotel list, but also a rating system which informs you about the facilities of each hotel and reflects the standards they are required to meet by the government. Because these authorities don't just represent one hotel chain or local interest, they generally have some incentive to be accurate and fair in their reports. Many state tourist offices have toll-free (800) numbers through which you can get this type of information in the U.S. Your travel agent can help you locate foreign tourist offices in the U.S.

Study a map. Find the exact location of the hotels you're considering. Don't assume that the hotel described in a guidebook as "centrally located" will be convenient to the museums. It might be next to the train station and the red light district.

Consult local tourist authorities while you're on the road. If you haven't reserved all of your hotels ahead of time,

---

check in with the Chamber of Commerce, tourist information bureau or the equivalent when you arrive at your destination. In Europe and some other parts of the world many
tourist authorities provide assistance in booking hotels or
pensions as well as excellent information on local attractions. Some will even cash travelers checks.

When purchasing a vacation "package" which includes
one or more hotels, get as much information as possible
from your travel agent before paying. Don't be satisfied with
a statement that you'll be staying in the "Central Hotel or
the equivalent." Learn the names of the hotels you'll be in,
what the travel agent knows about them, and what the
guidebooks say about them. See Chapter Ten, "Your Rights
as a Travel Consumer," for information on what to do if you
have any question about the reliability of the travel agent
or if the hotel doesn't deliver what was promised.

TRAVELER'S CHECKLIST
HOTELS

●●●●●●●●●●●●●●●●●●●●●●●●●●●●●●●●

☐ **1.** Bring along vouchers, information on hotels.

☐ **2.** Check hotel locations on map for convenience and safety.

☐ **3.** Pack a guidebook or name of "fallback" hotel in case reservation doesn't materialize.

_____

_____

_____

_____

_____

_____

_____

_____

_____

_____

_____

_____

_____

_____

Chapter Four

WHAT KIND OF LUGGAGE AND HOW TO PACK IT

"**W**hy do you have two suitcases?" asked my friend as we arrived at the airport for my departure to Peru and Ecuador. "Defensive packing," I replied. My friend looked at me blankly.

I pointed to the blue suitcase which I would not check. "This contains everything I need to survive for several days around Lima, where it's warm—bathing suit, cotton clothing and sandals."

I pointed to my second bag, which I was dispatching to the airplane's hold. "And this one contains blue jeans, hiking shoes, wool socks and sweaters—mountain clothes for a visit to Cuzco and Macchu Picchu."

"If the bag I check doesn't arrive with me, at least I'll be able to get along without it for a few days," I explained.

Never had my instincts for disaster been better. The bag I carried on the plane arrived with me. The bag I checked arrived several days later.

Meanwhile I went to the beach, visited the local sights and dined in one of the city's best restaurants—appropriately attired for each occasion.

Deciding which bags to carry on an airplane and which to check is only one in a long chain of decisions the traveler must make about luggage and packing for a trip. The chain begins with a decision about what type of suitcase or bag to buy. Then there's what to put in it each time you go and, if you're traveling by airplane, whether to check it or carry it on.

Once you have the bag to work with, then the questions revolve around what to take, how much to take, and how to pack the contents of the bag so that they will suffer the least wrinkling or breakage.

What should you consider in purchasing luggage?

The purpose and nature of your travel are the most important factors in determining what type of luggage to buy.

Is most of your travel for business? Or is it mostly for vacation? Are the business trips short, overnight hops or two-week international odysseys requiring many stops? Do you vacation at elegant Caribbean resorts where the suitcase will spend the week in the closet? Or is your idea of a vacation a camping trip or a mountain climb?

Although it may be tempting to base a suitcase purchase on stylistic factors such as color and shape, the answers to the above questions will be a more important guide to the type of luggage which makes sense for you.

Purchasing Luggage: What should you look for?

If you take trips of varying lengths, you may need a "wardrobe" of smaller bags which can be used individually or together—e.g., a garment bag, a medium-sized suitcase, a carry-on. If you tend to take long trips, one large bag and a small carry-on may be sufficient.

If you fly a lot, be sure to check the airlines' size and weight requirements before making your purchase.

Whenever possible, try to choose luggage which you can carry yourself or with a wheeled, collapsible luggage carrier. Very heavy, large or awkwardly shaped pieces can both slow down the pace and increase the temperature of the fast-moving traveler—especially when no porters or skycaps can be found.

The multi-purpose traveler may want to consider the dual personality nylon bags now sold by many camping and wilderness travel outfitters. For business trips, the bag can be used as a suitcase and carried in your hand. For more rugged environments, the suitcase converts to a pack which you can carry on your back.

The type of material you choose will affect the durability and portability—how light it is—of your luggage.

Leather and aluminum are the most durable materials, but they are also the most expensive. Both are also heavier than the nylon "soft-sided" bags which come in many shapes and sizes. (An aluminum suitcase saved at least one traveler's life, a luggage store clerk recounted. The traveler was on a boat which capsized. By clinging to the suitcase he was able to float until help arrived.)

For more normal travel conditions the challenge is to find a material which cannot be torn, ripped or punctured either by baggage handlers or machines, or by someone who may want to make off with the contents. Experts say that soft-sided luggage—virtually always lighter than leather or aluminum—can be just as durable as the hard-sided version if it's properly packed. Ballistic, Cordura and Oxford are all types of nylon used to make suitcases and camping gear. Ballistic nylon is the toughest material, but also the heaviest. Experts say that Cordura is twice as durable as Oxford nylon.

Trying to answer the question, "How soft is soft [luggage]?" *Consumer Reports* magazine identified and tested three types of "soft luggage" for a 1985 article. The magazine found that bags with no interior frame can be squashed and stored easily, but unless they're filled to the brim for travel, contents may slide around inside. "Partial-frame" and "full-frame" bags contain different types of internal supports which determine their rigidity, the most important factor in protecting your belongings. "You can do a quick in-store check of a soft-sider's rigidity," the magazine advises," by pressing firmly, then releasing, the bag's top sides and corners. The less it yields and the faster it rebounds, the more protection it's likely to offer," concluded the article.

Before buying, you should also consider several design elements. Does the bag contain inside or outside pockets or compartments? Are there inside straps or ribbons to secure the contents? Both packing and finding the socks or the bathrobe you're looking for later will be much easier if your belongings can be stowed in separate compartments.

Before going to shop, make a checklist of features to consider for your new bag. Consider purchasing a suitcase with wheels. Many travelers have found this a solution to the problem of the paucity of luggage carts or porters in many railroad stations and airports.

Are shoulder straps well mounted with, as the Luggage and Leather Goods Information Bureau recommends, "metal, or metal-reinforced bases with a number of rivets, screws or prongs attached to the frame of the case itself"? Can the bag be locked? What type of lock do you prefer? *Consumer Reports* magazine suggests that when choosing carry-on luggage you give special attention to handles and shoulder straps, zippers, and ability of the bag to withstand rain. They also suggest that you consider purchasing a bag with a "rigid floor that folds (which) can be compressed for storage."

What to Take Along

"Travel light" is the most time-honored advice offered to travelers. But is it either possible or desirable?

Now we enter a realm in which personal tastes and prejudices must be balanced with practical considerations. Is it better to carry a lighter bag, and then feel uncomfortable wearing your one light cotton "all-purpose" dress when you're unexpectedly invited to dine in an elegant restaurant?

What if the one pair of shoes you bring along gets rained on or a heel breaks? If there's a 50 percent chance of rain during your trip, do you want to chance not having a raincoat?

Here are some things to keep in mind as you plan what to take:

Excess baggage: This can be a hassle if you're traveling by air. Not only can it be difficult to carry, but too-large or heavy carry-on luggage can be a hazard in airplane cabins for passengers and flight attendants. Check the baggage limits—especially the recently changed, stricter ones for carry-on bags—for your flights before you pack. These will vary depending on whether your flight is domestic or international, and depending on the size of the planes in which you'll fly. If you're going to take domestic flights on overseas airlines, the limits could vary from those for the international flight. The bag you can hand-carry on an Iberia (the Spanish international airline) trans-Atlantic flight, for example, many times will not fit in the cabin on planes used by the Spanish domestic airline, Avianca.

Length of the trip: If you'll only be away a couple of days, you can probably opt on the light side in every category from clothing to reading material to toiletries. As a frequent traveler, I have two toiletry kits—one with toothbrush, toothpaste, prescription drugs and a few other essentials which I keep in my carry-on luggage; and a larger one stocked with my mini-first aid kit and items such as cold tablets, a long-term supply of my favorite shampoo and other items which are non-essential but nice to have on a longer trip.

Destination(s): If you're spending a month in a major city anywhere, don't worry about running out of toothpaste—or even about needing an extra T-shirt or pair of shoes. All of these things will be readily available at your destination.

For a safari vacation or a trek through the Himalayas, however, you'll want to have all your necessities in the bag.

Activities: This will determine how much and what type of clothing to bring. In general, look for wrinkle-proof fabrics and streamlined styles. If the destination is Moscow in January, consider items such as a down vest, which can be rolled into a compact package and by definition is never wrinkled. Look for "mix 'n match" wardrobe components. Women can choose a suit which, with a tailored blouse, serves for daytime business but with a silk blouse is appropriate for evening wear.

Accommodations: Travelers who stay in "business" hotels can generally have laundry or cleaning done quickly. But if you're traveling on a tight budget or spending a lot of time in a not-so-cosmopolitan international capital, try to bring clothing you can wash out and dry quickly in your room.

For these kinds of trips, consider packing a stretchable clothes line, available in many notions departments, and some hanger-topped clothespins which allow you to suspend laundry from doorknobs or towel hooks to dry, and possibly a small travel iron. (Be sure to check the type of electrical current in the country where you'll be traveling, and if necessary, equip yourself with an adapter or converter for the iron.)

If you'll be staying in very basic hotels, or in accommodations such as a safari camp, some other almost weightless items which might prove useful in the hotel or on the road are a Swiss army knife with corkscrew, scissors and other gadgets, a battery-powered reading light which you clip onto a book, and a small flashlight.

Bringing home purchases: If you expect to be bringing home souvenirs or other purchases from abroad, you might consider packing a collapsible bag in your luggage.

And finally, review what you plan to take. Will it really fit in your luggage, and do you really need it?

How to Pack

The secret is to compartmentalize the components of your luggage. The goals should be to find what you need easily, to preserve clothing in as close to wearable condition as possible, and to be able to repack easily.

First things first. The Air Transport Association says that 99 percent of the 675 million bags checked on U.S. airlines in 1987 arrived without incident. One thing you can do to keep your luggage out of the other one percent is to make sure it's tagged outside and inside. (If you're a business executive who has reason to be concerned about terrorism, get luggage tags which do not display your name to all oglers.) Remove old airline destination tags—they may result in misrouting of the bags.

Start by placing all the items you want to pack on your bed, so you can be guided by a visual impression of what you'll be taking along. This will help you pack more systematically and neatly.

"Package" the contents of your suitcase. Place all the socks in one bag or compartment, underwear in another, pajamas and bathrobe in another. Then you won't have to overturn the whole heap to get dressed every morning.

To minimize wrinkling, pack shirts, blouses, sweaters, slacks and even jackets or dresses in plastic bags or separate them by layers of plastic or tissue paper. Pack extra plastic bags for laundry, shoes or additional purchases.

Consider investing in a "travel organizer" which contains three compartments for toiletries. The organizer can be hung from a bathroom hook on a strap and folded into a compact unit inside your suitcase. If at least one of the compartments is clear plastic, you'll be able to find the toothpaste without emptying out all the contents. Larger versions equipped with a hanger at the top serve well for lingerie, hosiery, jewelry and other small items.

Pack essential or valuable items in a carry-on bag and keep it with you at all times. Your list of essentials should include prescription drugs, extra glasses, travel documents and money, and the papers needed for business meetings. Valuables you should not entrust to others include jewelry, computers and photographic equipment.

Frequent travelers may want to invest in a carry-on or other small suitcase which is packed and ready to go at all times. Among the items to keep in it are a set of toiletries, prescriptions, overnight gear and underwear.

Pack defensively. If you're staying away overnight, pack not only the above essentials but also toiletries and a day's change of clothes in a carry-on bag. If your bag is lost in transit, you'll at least be able to alternate between the two outfits until your clothes arrive or you can purchase replacements.

Planning

In order to avoid luggage hassles while traveling, do some advance research.

Know the airline's baggage allowance. Although this doesn't happen often while traveling in the U.S., you may be required to pay an excess baggage charge if you exceed the allowance while traveling overseas. The allowance may change depending on which airline you fly. As a frequent traveler to Spain, I'd never had trouble staying within the allowance for my trans-Atlantic flights. Once, however, I stopped over in London before going on to the Spanish island of Menorca. Not thinking ahead, I checked my bags from the U.S. only as far as London. When I checked in at the London airport a few hours later for my connecting flight to Spain, the airline wanted to charge me for excess weight.

Luggage checked all the way through from the U.S. to Menorca would not have been subject to the excess baggage requirement. Inside Europe, however, rules are stricter and the penalty you pay for carrying excess baggage, even on a short flight, can be costly.

When you make airplane reservations for an international trip, ask the reservations clerk or travel agent to check on baggage limits for you so that you can pack accordingly. Some airlines will provide you with a brochure that explains their baggage allowances.

Get information about handling awkward or delicate baggage—skis or the carton of family china—before you report to the airport or train station.

Try to learn about the facilities and layout of the airport or train station where you'll be arriving. Your travel agent or airline reservations clerk may be able to help. Some trains or railroad terminals have luggage carts for the public. Others do not.

Decide which luggage you want to check BEFORE you pack. This will determine what goes in which bag, and which bags you'll take.

Inform yourself about baggage insurance. You may already be covered for loss or damage to your luggage by a household policy. Airline companies are required to assume liability of up to $1,250 for loss, delay or damage to bags on domestic flights in 1988. Liability rates may differ for international flights. Supplementary coverage may also be provided if you have purchased your ticket through American Express or certain other credit card companies.

In all cases, make a list of valuables so that you have a record should any of them disappear or be damaged.

Carry a couple of shock cords. These tough elastic cords

with hooks at both ends are the perfect temporary remedy for a suitcase which suffers a broken lock and flies open in transit. To keep the bag closed, just wrap cords around it and secure them.

The Bottom Line

Last, but not least, while you're traveling: WATCH YOUR LUGGAGE.

Traveling in a remote South Pacific nation I narrowly avoided losing my luggage not once but twice in two days by following this advice. In the first case, I had about an hour's layover between flights at a tiny airport in a small town. Killing time waiting for the second flight, I examined my baggage tag and realized that the luggage was programmed to go to the wrong destination. I called it to the attention of the agent just as the bag was being lifted into the hold of a departing plane. He sprinted outside and retrieved it with only minutes to spare.

On the second occasion, I checked in and noticed that the agent had kept the suitcase next to him, rather than putting it on the luggage truck. When boarding time came, the suitcase was still at the counter. As I entered the plane, I told the steward: "My bag is still in the airport. Please don't take off without it." Watching from the door of the plane as preparations were made for take-off, at the eleventh hour I said to the steward: "My bag's still not here. Please have someone go get it."

He did, and everything arrived intact—at the same time I did.

Even better than watching your luggage, keep your hands on it if possible. The airlines often advise: "The luggage you carry will arrive with you." But whether you're carrying it or checking it, keep an eye on all of your luggage constantly. There are an infinite number of places and ways to lose all this stuff which you have so carefully selected and determined was important to bring along. Here are some lessons I've learned:

■ Count the number of bags you're carrying—including a purse or shopping bag or whatever—and check frequently to make sure you have them all.

■ If you're traveling with one or more other persons, agree that someone will always be responsible for watching the bags. For example, when the taxi pulls up to the train station or airport door, one person should watch as the bags are unloaded and count them before the taxi drives off. If you're arriving in a strange place, put one person in a corner with all the bags while another goes to look for the check-in counter or the bus or whatever.

■ When you check bags at an airport, make sure that the airline personnel actually put the bag on the conveyor belt or wherever it must be picked up.

■ If your bags have been checked, don't delay in picking them up at your destination. In some airports and train stations, there is little or no security to protect them.

■ A final caution: Never travel with luggage or packages given to you by strangers. One unfortunate young U.S. citizen was sentenced to several years in a Spanish prison because the suitcase he agreed to carry over the border for someone had a false bottom concealing a load of cocaine.

TRAVELER'S CHECKLIST
BAGGAGE

•••••••••••••••••••••••••••••••••••••

☐ **1.** Check luggage size, weight, strength for this trip.

☐ **2.** Learn about carry-on and other restrictions on baggage.

☐ **3.** Check on charges for excess weight on airplanes.

☐ **4.** Bring a luggage cart.

☐ **5.** Protect contents of luggage against theft with locks.

☐ **6.** Put identification tags inside and outside luggage.

☐ **7.** Pack small bag with essential items to carry at all times.

_____

_____

_____

_____

_____

_____

_____

_____

Chapter Five
MONEY MATTERS

I'd been warned in Peru that the vibrant, colorful market across the street from the train station in Cuzco was a notorious site for thefts.

Warily snapping photos of the vendors in their bright clothing, I scrunched my purse tightly between my right elbow and my ribs. Finishing the pictures, I carefully inserted the camera into my purse—continuing to hug it to my body—in order to enter and explore the indoor market.

The indoor market was dim and the aisles were crowded. Before I knew what had happened, I was surrounded by a ring of menacing little boys—perhaps eight to ten years old—who wouldn't let me pass. Seconds later, I read on the face of one the women fruit vendors that something had happened. The little boys were gone, my parachute nylon purse had been sliced open with a knife or similar object, and the camera had disappeared. Luckily, my money and passport were still inside.

Knowing there was no chance I'd see my Pentax again, I made the obligatory reports to the police, stuffed the forms they gave me into my bag, and proceeded with my travels.

On my return, I filed a claim, and a few weeks later, my insurance company sent me a check to cover the cost of purchasing a similar camera.

The relationship between travel and money is much broader than merely the cash or credit cards we need to pay for our meals and hotel. As in the case of the camera theft, there are other elements which may become evident only after a crisis or disaster.

Insurance

Insurance coverage is a case in point. Insurance will only be a help to you if you think about it BEFORE you go.

Offers of policies which claim they'll bail you out of travel disasters seem to arrive in the mail almost daily. Come-ons for health and accident coverage, car rental insurance, baggage insurance, insurance against delay, cancellation or interruption of a trip pile up on the desk of anyone who has a credit card. Experts say rule number one when considering such offers is to examine the coverage you already have.

Health Insurance: In most cases "a person who has health insurance already has coverage while traveling," explains Amy Biderman, Manager of Media Information for the Health Insurance Association of America. Travelers should realize that if they incur medical expenses while away from home, "generally the doctor or hospital will want to be paid up front," Biderman warned. But in most cases, she said, if you present the receipts to your regular insurance company, you'll receive the normal reimbursement. (Be sure to calculate the current exchange rate and record it so that you can translate your claim into dollars later.) If you're a traveler, ask your insurance company about coverage before signing on the dotted line. Be aware that HMO's are less likely than regular insurance plans to offer coverage while you're away from home.

What about supplemental health insurance being offered to travelers by various organizations and credit card companies? Biderman advises that such policies "would not necessarily be a good buy" if you already have good basic coverage. Retired persons should be aware, however, that Medicare does not pay for medical expenses incurred outside the U.S. and that they will need some additional coverage.

A special caveat to travelers who purchase insurance to

cover medical emergencies or trip cancellation: before buying, check to see who determines whether an early return was in fact a "medical emergency." Policies which specify that the airline, rather than a doctor, decides could leave you unprotected.

Car Insurance: Your own car insurance may also apply if you have an accident with a rental car. If you're using the car on business, your company may be covering you with its insurance. "If you add these two factors together the majority of travelers do not need the additional coverage which is offered by car rental companies," observes Mark Rosenberg, Vice President for Federal Affairs of the Insurance Information Institute in Washington, DC.

Baggage Insurance: Policies which claim to cover the cost of lost or damaged baggage and its contents may also duplicate automatic coverage which comes with your airline ticket, or coverage by your homeowner's insurance policy, cautioned Rosenberg. Purchase of an airline ticket carries with it coverage of up to $1,250 for damage or loss of your luggage or its contents as long as it's in the custody of the airline.

"A homeowner's policy covers the contents of your home, even while you're traveling," explains Rosenberg. "If your car is broken into while you are traveling and your luggage is stolen, it should be covered." He issues two caveats with regard to coverage by homeowner insurance. One is that jewelry, furs and other items of extraordinary value must be identified and listed separately on your policy. The other is that normally such policies do NOT cover "anything for the production of income," such as a secretary's or executive's laptop computer or a movie maker's cameras. Special coverage must be sought for these items.

Flight or Tour Cancellation and Delay Insurance: One habit which will protect the contents of your pocketbook in general, as well as with regard to insurance, is to always ask about the penalties you'll incur for canceling or changing a flight on your airline ticket. If your ticket prohibits any changes, you could end up paying the same fare for a one-way return from London as you paid for the original round trip "bargain" ticket. Does the possibility that you'll need to make such changes justify buying insurance to cover them?

Trip cancellation or interruption insurance is available from Travel Guard International through travel agents, and is recommended by the American Society of Travel Agents. It provides for reimbursement of your deposit if you have to cancel a trip; as well as for expenses incurred if an emergency requires you to cut the trip short.

This type of insurance can be purchased from Travel Guard as part of a package which also includes coverage for emergency and medical assistance and loss of baggage. Coverage is for one trip only. Frequent travelers should be particularly careful about scrutinizing their existing policies before paying an additional premium for separate coverage of each trip. Travel Guard can be reached by a calling a toll-free number: (800) 782-5151.

Foreign Currency

If your trip takes you out of the U.S., and especially if your destination is far-flung or your journey is an extended one, inform yourself about the currency regulations of your destination before you go.

It generally is useful to arrive in a foreign country carrying a small quantity of the local currency which will cover phone calls, taxi fares and other incidentals, especially if your flight arrives at the airport in the middle of the night when the bank is closed. I have found that the smaller and more exotic my point of entry into a country, the more likely that the airport bank will be closed even during part of the day.

In the U.S., you can locate a foreign exchange dealer in big cities by looking in the yellow pages. Another place where you can sometimes buy currency is at a main office or large branch of a major local bank. International airports in the U.S. usually have currency exchanges too, but if you're traveling at odd hours, don't count on finding them open.

Every country has its own idiosyncratic rules about money. If you are going to Switzerland to empty out your secret bank account, be prepared to file U.S. Customs Form 4790, required for bringing the equivalent of $10,000 or more into the U.S. from any other country. The currency is not dutiable, but failure to file the form can result in both civil and criminal penalties.

If you're going to a country in Eastern Europe or others such as Burma where movement of foreign currency is rigidly controlled, be prepared to fill out a form declaring every penny you have brought. You may be required to carry a currency declaration form at all times and to have hotel and other financial transactions recorded on it. Don't lose the form, because you will be expected to turn it in when you leave the country. And if you're tempted by offers to change your dollars on the black market, just remember that U.S. citizens are subject to local laws; there's little anyone can do to help you if you are caught violating them.

Cash, Credit Cards and Travelers Checks

The BankCard Holders of America (BCA), a consumer group, recommends that you carry some of each when you travel.

Credit cards contribute to your financial health by providing a float—the gap between the time you incur the expense and the time it's actually charged to you. Where credit cards are accepted, they may be particularly advantageous for transactions in remote parts of the world where it takes longer to process your expenditure. Sometimes an airline ticket or meal charged to your card doesn't show up for months. With computerization, however, the credit card companies are becoming much more efficient.

If the value of the dollar is declining, this technique could cost you money. Also, although you'll find establishments which accept credit cards in major cities anywhere in the world, the cards will not be much help if you're canoeing down the Amazon or trekking through the Himalayas. In these cases, make sure that you're carrying the local currency.

Another caveat for credit card-users is that some hotels

How to Plan a Successful Trip

freeze a portion of your credit reserve when you register and give them an imprint of the plastic. Since the size of the freeze—which may be effective for up to 15 days—is based on the hotel's estimate of your final bill, it could be larger than the amount you actually spend.

The Wall Street Journal reported the experience of one business traveler who was unaware of this practice. When the time came to pay a car rental bill with a credit card, he found that both his Mastercard and Visa accounts were frozen—even though the bills he'd incurred were under his credit limit. Before you register, ask the hotel clerk to tell you if the hotel's policy is to freeze credit, and how much they intend to freeze. If you're planning a long, expensive trip be sure to bring along some method of payment—probably travelers checks—other than the credit card.

The BCA cautions about approaches by insurers who say they will protect your liability in the case of a credit card loss. According to BCA, under federal law your liability is limited to $50 if you immediately report a loss or theft, so there is no need to insure yourself for amounts beyond that.

BCA points out the advantage of using travelers checks for your daily expenses is that they can be traced and you can receive reimbursement if they are lost. Note that, if you shop around, you can probably find a local bank or currency exchange which sells travelers checks without charging a commission.

Another way to save on your travelers checks is to purchase them in a foreign currency. It might save you from paying a service charge when cashing them abroad. Foreign currency travelers checks are widely available at banks in major cities and at currency exchanges in airports.

Once you've arrived overseas, you'll generally pay a higher commission to change money in your hotel or in a shop or restaurant than at a bank or a currency exchange. Ask the bank or currency exchange if it offers different rates for cash than for travelers checks. Also ask whether the service charge is computed per transaction or according to the amount of money exchanged. If you expect to spend the money soon, you might save by cashing $100 at one time, instead of $50 twice.

Not all currency service charges are equal for all customers. If you're living or even just spending a few weeks or months in one location overseas, do your business with one bank regularly. You may find that this results in a lower rate for your transaction.

Financial Emergencies: At times it seems that the almighty credit card is the answer to almost any money problem. Your American Express and Diner's Club cards give you access to emergency cash in a variety of locations and systems, including check-cashing and automatic teller machines. With Visa and Master cards you can use Western Union's domestic and international cash transfer systems. (See box.).

Before going on a trip, secure information from each of your credit card companies about how to cancel the cards if they are lost or stolen. Be prepared for the worst by carrying a list of phone numbers and instructions with you.

SOURCES OF EMERGENCY CASH

Whether in the U.S. or overseas, travelers can choose from several services to obtain cash while away from home. Fees are charged for all of these services; the cost—as well as the amount of time it takes to actually get the money—can vary widely depending on where the sender and traveler are located. It may be necessary to check with one or more of these services to determine which is the cheapest, fastest way to get cash to a particular location. Finally, you should look into the procedures for obtaining money—and, if necessary, arrange for someone to send it to you—before you leave on your trip. Among the services through which you can obtain cash:

1. Credit cards: American Express and Diner's Club are among those which offer several ways to secure cash if you have an emergency while out of town. For details, call their (800) numbers before you leave on your trip.

(This list, along with your passport number and a copy of its first few pages, should be packed separately from your money and travel documents.)

If all the usual instruments for paying travel expenses fail you while overseas, the U.S. government reassures its citizens, "Should you become destitute . . . the American consul will help you get in touch with your family, friends, bank or employer and tell you how to arrange for them to send funds to you." Consular offices also have a small fund which can be used to tide over American citizens confronted with a financial emergency.

Security

One way to become destitute, of course, is to be robbed. An increasing number of hotels all over the world offer to

---

2. Western Union: Through the (800) number listed in your local phone directory, cash can be sent by wire 24 hours a day, 365 days a year using a Master or Visa card to points throughout the U.S. and about 75 foreign countries. If you prefer to pay in cash, you can do so at a Western Union office.

3. U.S. Postal Service: Money orders can be sent to both domestic and international destinations through the regular express mail system.

4. Foreign exchange dealers: Dealers such as Deak International sell bank drafts in foreign currency and send them overseas by overnight courier. Check your yellow pages for names of local dealers.

5. Banks: U.S. banks that have a relationship with a foreign bank can wire funds to you regardless of whether or not you have an account.

---

store your money and valuables in a secure box, and the offer should be accepted in most cases. However, not all storage facilities in all locations provide equal protection.

One offer I found very resistible was in a small hotel in Izmir, Turkey, where travelers' valuables were casually tossed into a drawer at the front desk along with the pencils and paper clips. Another offer I should have resisted, but didn't, was at a major Amsterdam hotel undergoing renovations which had upset its normal procedures. The safe deposit boxes were in a cubicle with a door the staff sometimes left open to the lobby. If I'd had a diamond tiara to stow away, any thief walking through could have grabbed it.

In both the U.S. and overseas, if you're in a hotel with a good security system, stow your extra money, airline tickets and other valuables there and only carry exactly what you need—perhaps cash and one credit card—while you're outside. Men should carry money and documents in inside pockets.

Women should consider carrying two travel purses. One, large enough to hold non-essential items such as make-up and maps as well as documents and money, should be made of strong material (preferably leather) and have secure fastenings on all compartments. I personally prefer a bag with at least one inside zipper compartment, in which I place money, credit cards and documents. Thus if I'm "pick-pocketed," it's possible that the most important items won't be stolen.

In addition, I always travel with a very small purse—preferably with a shoulder strap—which holds only the few necessities for a night on the town or for a shopping expedition to a busy, crowded market. I cross the strap over my shoulder diagonally, so the bag is attached to me securely; and sometimes keep the purse totally out of sight by wearing a jacket or coat over it.

In remote, rugged and/or dangerous areas both men and women may want to use a money belt or document wallet which can be hung around your neck or strapped to your leg.

Prime locations for losing or forgetting money or being robbed are shops, banks, airports—anywhere you have to pay for something. So don't hurry away after your transaction. Check to make sure you have the money, the credit card, your passport; and put the items in their proper place before venturing onto the street again.

As "insurance" against loss, leave a list of the numbers of your travelers checks, credit cards and airline tickets with someone at home; carry one yourself and if you're traveling with someone else, exchange lists.

Car Rental

Studies by Runzheimer Reports on Travel Management and others have documented major increases in car rental costs in recent years. Some of the measures which corporations are applying to reduce these costs can also be implemented by individual vacation travelers.

One is to learn how to read a car rental bill and contract, and to know where errors or misunderstandings are likely to occur. Publicized daily or weekly rental rates generally reflect only a portion of actual cost. Insurance and taxes—and sometimes, if you rent the car in one city and wish to return it in another, drop-off charges—must be added to get a full picture. In countries with a value added tax, your cost could leap dramatically because the tax could add as much as a third to the quoted rate.

Be sure to check your own or your company's car insurance coverage before deciding whether to opt for the insurance offered by the rental company. In many cases you'll find you're already covered adequately.

Another way to reduce car rental expenses generally is to return the vehicle with a full tank. If the tank isn't full when you received the car, return it filled to the same level. If you don't, you may be charged a fill-up at a rate which is inevitably higher than the one you'd pay down the street. (In some countries, rental companies are prohibited from charging you a higher rate for the fill-up.)

Taxes

The 1986 tax law made important changes with respect to deduction of business meals and entertainment and other travel-related expenses. Most important is that business meals

---

and entertainment expenses—previously 100 percent deductible—are now only 80 percent deductible. If you don't have a corporate travel department backing up your decisions on business travel expenses, check with your accountant or lawyer for details on new reporting requirements and on the fine points of deductibility of special travel expenses—e.g., cruises and out-of-town meetings—which have also been changed. And make a note that the expenses of educational travel related to your work may not be deducted at all now.

TRAVELER'S CHECKLIST
MONEY
....

☐ **1.** Buy travelers checks and foreign currency, if necessary.

☐ **2.** Bring along necessary credit cards, personal checks.

☐ **3.** Leave a copy of numbers of travelers checks, credit cards, etc. at home. Give one to traveling companion.

☐ **4.** Find out what to do about lost or stolen travelers checks or credit cards.

☐ **5.** Bring along information on how to secure emergency cash.

☐ **6.** Check adequacy of all insurance coverage. Buy more if necessary.

_____

_____

_____

_____

_____

_____

_____

_____

_____

Chapter Six

YOUR HEALTH AND SAFETY

When you consider all the things that can happen to your body while you're traveling, it's enough to make you want to stay at home.

In twenty years of travel throughout the world I have endured excruciatingly painful but minor surgery to remove more than a dozen sea urchin spines from a foot and a finger while on the Greek island of Crete; stomach cramps—diagnosed and successfully treated as amoebic dysentery—which sent me to a medical clinic instead of across the Khyber Pass from Afghanistan into Pakistan; and hours of stabbing pain and loss of hearing while flying from La Paz, Bolivia back to the U.S.—caused by flying when I had a sinus infection.

I consider myself lucky that these are the worst health problems I've encountered in the jungles, deserts and remote mountain areas where I've traveled.

It's pretty hard to see a sea urchin before it stings you; and traveling in certain countries you're likely to contract stomach or intestinal problems no matter what you eat. So anticipation may not have prevented these unpleasant episodes.

But I could have avoided the agony of the flight from La Paz to the States if I'd been better informed about the risks of flying in an airplane when when your sinuses are congested. A British medical journal, *the Lancet*, points out,

"The ill-prepared traveler is likely to figure among the 50 percent of international travelers who experience some kind of adverse effect on their health" as the result of a trip.

When preparing for a distant trip, most of us think first of prevention against tropical or infectious diseases such as malaria, cholera or yellow fever. But a recent analysis of deaths of American males while traveling abroad shows that the more serious threats are the ones which by comparison seem more mundane—cardiovascular disease, injuries from automobiles and motorcycle accidents, and drowning.

The study, which was conducted by Stephen W. Hargarten, M.D., of St. Luke's Hospital in Milwaukee, Wis. found that 72.8 percent of the persons who died in the two years studied were men, and that nearly half of them—49 percent—died of cardiovascular diseases. Injuries, the second most common cause of death, accounted for 22 percent. Infectious diseases were the cause of death in less than two percent of the cases reported.

Information is an important tool in preventing health problems while traveling. Taking time before departure to learn which immunizations to get, what type of anti-malaria pill to take, what food and drink to consume or avoid, and how to secure help in a crisis could literally save your life—and might even save your trip.

But the Hargarten study suggests two important additional preventive measures to consider:

■ If you have a chronic condition, especially heart disease, make sure that the itinerary and change of environment will not create more stress than you can handle;

■ Stay alert to the possibility of accidents, both in planning the trip and once you're in an unfamiliar setting.

Here are some tips on how to stay healthy on the road.

For All Travelers:

■ Obtain up to date information on health problems in the destinations on your itinerary;

■ Prevent jet lag (see Chapter Seven, "How to Prevent Jet

Lag,") and general fatigue which make you more suscep-
tible to illness;

■ Be alert to the danger of accidents. Motor vehicle accidents, drownings and similar mishaps are a greater risk
when you're in unfamiliar territory. Important preventive
measures, Hargarten says, include wearing a helmet while
riding a motorcycle or other light vehicle; whenever possible, wearing a seatbelt in a car or truck; choosing swimming areas carefully, and avoiding use of alcohol while
swimming;

■ Pack an extra set of glasses so that you will be spared
the frustration of going without them if you lose or break
your regular pair. This is particularly important if you're
going to a remote area where it may be difficult to have new
glasses made. If your itinerary requires constant moving
around, loss of your glasses may require an unwanted delay
while you wait for a new pair to be made.

AIDS Update

AIDS has become a major concern for world travelers.
Information on its prevalence and research results are
changing rapidly. Before visiting any area where AIDS could
be a particular concern—such as Africa or Haiti—check
with your local health department or the Travelers Health
Section of the federal government's Center for Disease Control in Atlanta. The telephone number is (404) 329-2572.

In general, risk of AIDS arises from sexual intercourse
with partners in high-risk groups, from non-sterile needles
or syringes (such as those shared by drug users) or from
contaminated blood supplies. It is known that many countries do not report complete data on AIDS incidence and
data on which countries screen blood plasma for transfusions is also not up to date. Experts do not recommend that
you cancel a trip to a location with a high incidence of AIDS,
but they suggest the following precautions:

■ "Diabetics and other persons who require routine in-
jections should carry with them a supply of syringes and

needles sufficient to last their entire stay abroad," says the Center for Disease Control. Be aware, however, that in some countries it might be illegal to carry these items without a prescription.

■ If you unexpectedly require an injection while traveling, make sure that the needle and syringe come from a sterile package or that they have been sterilized with chemicals or boiled for 20 minutes.

■ If you need a transfusion overseas, check with the Red Cross or with U.S. or other Western embassies for guidance on how to find a safe source.

■ Acupuncture and tattooing instruments as well as dentists' tools should be sterilized between uses. Don't take a chance if you're not sure they have been sterilized.

■ Some countries require testing for AIDS of some or all visitors. Be sure to check on this when you get a visa.

For Isolated or Risky International Destinations

Talk to or visit your doctor to make sure that you are informed about the health problems of the area you're visiting and to get advice on how to reduce your risk of becoming ill.

If you're taking a long trip or going to distant, exotic points and/or if you have chronic health problems, consider having a check-up. "Special precautions are necessary for those with allergies, gastro-intestinal conditions, diabetes, cardiovascular or pulmonary disease," suggests Martin S. Wolfe, Director of Traveler's Medical Service in Washington, D.C.

Discuss the details of your itinerary with your doctor. Simply living with a different language, culture or physical environment adds stress to daily life. Will the trip create additional physical or mental stress by requiring more walking or climbing or less sleep or a more rigid routine than you're used to?

Get the recommended or required inoculations. Your local health department can provide this information. (See appendix for names of publications that can help identify which inoculations you'll need.) In talking to your health department or your doctor, ask what is recommended as well as what is required. The fact that a foreign country does not require you to be inoculated against a particular disease does not mean that there is no danger of contracting it.

Smallpox is considered to have been eradicated, and the vaccination is no longer recommended for travel anywhere in the world. Shots for diseases such as cholera, yellow fever and plague may be recommended, especially if you will be visiting remote areas in affected countries. Be aware that because of the delicacy of the vaccine, yellow fever immunizations cannot be administered by your doctor. For information on where and when the shots are scheduled, contact your local health department.

If you're going to the Third World, your doctor may also recommend a gamma globulin shot for short-term protection against hepatitis and will probably suggest that "childhood" immunizations such as tetanus and polio be brought up to date.

If necessary, undertake an anti-malaria regimen. You will need to start taking the drug before your arrival in the affected area.   Spread by mosquitoes, malaria remains a risk in tropical regions. Despite advances toward a vaccine, "the mosquitoes and the disease are winning the war. They're making an excellent counter-attack [against preventive measures] and in previously affected areas it's increasing," says Dr. Ronald St. John of the World Health Organization.

In some areas malaria has become resistant to chloroquine, the drug most commonly prescribed in the past. The U.S. government's "Health Information" pamphlet (cited in the appendix) provides country-by-country information on the type of regimen recommended.

If you're going to a high-risk area—for example on a camping or safari trip—equip yourself with mosquito repellent. And because most insect bites occur between dusk and dawn, use mosquito netting for sleeping.

Bring along prescription drugs you know you'll need. Because of the variation in the nature of drugs and drug laws throughout the world, it's best to bring along a complete supply of prescription drugs you take regularly. Be sure to carry them in properly labeled bottles, so as not to raise the suspicions of overseas customs authorities. Also ask your doctor to write a prescription for extra quantities, just in case you lose the supply you've brought along.

In some countries drugs sold by prescription in the U.S. are sold over the counter. In others, these drugs may not be available at all. Drug names and exact contents may differ and the containers may lack warning labels or instructions. Thus it is safer to bring along items such as insulin for diabetics and an adrenalin kit for persons with severe allergies to insect stings, as well as medications you take routinely.

Watch what you eat and drink.

"Traveler's diarrhea," the most common disease of travelers, can be prevented most effectively by avoiding raw or unpeeled foods and contaminated water. The juicy slice of papaya which has been reposing on the street vendor's stand for hours, the attractive lettuce salad which may have been washed in contaminated water, and the ice in your cocktail can ultimately cause you more misery than the immediate pleasure of consuming them.

Although scientists have been working on preventive anti-diarrhea drugs, these are generally not recommended because of their side effects and because they may destroy organisms required to protect your body from other diseases.

The greatest danger from traveler's diarrhea is dehydration, so if you contract the disease treat it with large doses of non-caffeinated, non-acidic fluids such as fruit juices, soft drinks, or thin soup and salted crackers to replace lost salt.

"Traveler's diarrhea is usually a mild, self-limiting disorder, with complete recovery even in the absence of therapy," according to the National Institutes of Health, "hence therapy should be considered optional." If diarrhea persists, see a doctor to ascertain whether you have contracted a more serious disease.

Bring along a medical kit.

Dr. Wolfe suggests that it include a thermometer, bandages and gauze, adhesive tape, an antiseptic or bactericidal soap solution, aspirin, antacids, and an anti-motion sickness drug. If you're flying, bring a nasal decongestant and possibly nose drops. Travelers who suffer from allergies should take an antihistamine. He also recommends taking a non-narcotic pain medication and, for hot climates, salt tablets. If you're prone to sprained ankles and similar injuries, include an elastic bandage.

If you'll be traveling in very remote areas, ask your doctor whether you should take along a broad-spectrum antibiotic in case of emergency.

Have a dental check-up before you leave. Make it a rule to check out and have treatment for any dental problems before going on an extended trip. Ask your dentist how to relieve a toothache or what to do about a lost filling. You can also assemble your own dental care kit to use in emergencies.

For toothache relief, the American Dental Association recommends rinsing your mouth vigorously with warm water to clean out any debris, then using dental floss to remove any trapped food. Do not put heat or aspirin on the tooth or gums. An application of oil of cloves—available in drug stores—to the affected tooth can relieve the pain.

A longer-term stopgap until you can get to a dentist is to make a paste of three drops of clove oil and a small amount of zinc oxide powder (also available in drug stores), dry the cavity well with cotton and have someone help you fill it tightly with the paste. After ten minutes it will harden and provide a temporary filling.

Coping With Medical Emergencies Overseas

The best advice for coping with medical emergencies is to anticipate them. If you have a chronic problem, inform yourself ahead of time about the availability of transfusions, emergency equipment or other special services you might require. Ask your doctor to help you do this, or contact one of the international medical organizations listed separately in this chapter.

Bring along the address and phone number of the U.S. embassy and consulates in countries you'll be visiting. Should you or a traveling companion require emergency evacuation or other special medical assistance, the U.S. embassy or consulate can advise you about what to do. They can also help you find an English-speaking doctor.

Before departure, check to see whether your medical insurance covers overseas expenses. If not, you may want to consider taking out short-term coverage from an organization such as those listed separately in this chapter. (For further details on health insurance for travelers see Chapter Five, "Money Matters.")

Carry with you medical histories and any other information which would be needed by a doctor in case of emergency, especially if you have a chronic condition or drug or other potentially life-threatening allergies.

Traveling Safely

The traveler's body is vulnerable not only to germs, jet lag and stress, but also to sudden, unexpected assaults or violence.

To maximize your prospects of returning home safely from a trip, consider these safety points before you go and keep them in mind while you're on the road.

Check your hotel room and floor for information on fire exits, fire alarms, and other safety features. A State Department pamphlet suggests that travelers kill two birds with one stone by booking a hotel room on the seventh floor. This level is high enough to protect you from outside intruders, the pamphlet suggests, but low enough to be reached by fire equipment.

Be aware of hotel security or lack of it. Years ago I made a reservation and spent one night in a moderately priced hotel in downtown Bangkok. As I stumbled groggily, just off my flight, into the elevator and up to my room, I didn't know whether to be relieved or scared stiff by the armed guards who were stationed prominently on each floor. On the wall in the room was a threatening list of the costs which would be incurred by guests whose rooms were found to lack sheets, towels, waste baskets or furniture when they checked out.

I could only surmise that these precautions were taken

because of a history or at least a threat of violence and theft occurring in the hotel.

This experience reinforced for me the importance of checking up on both the neighborhood and the hotel before deciding to sleep there. Determine whether the hotel is in a neighborhood where you can walk around safely, especially if you're in a city.

When you check in, make sure you are escorted to your room by a porter who checks to make sure no one is hiding

---

MEDICAL SERVICES FOR TRAVELERS

The following organizations offer a range of medical services to travelers including emergency evacuation and some supplementary insurance coverage. For information on services and membership, contact:

■ **Access America Hotline**, a subsidiary of Blue Cross Blue Shield, 600 Third Ave., Box 807, New York, NY 10163. Phone is (800) 851-2800.

■ **International Association of Medical Assistance to Travelers,** 417 Center St., Lewiston, NY 14092. Phone is (716) 754-4883.

■ **International SOS Assistance**, P.O. Box 11568, Philadelphia, PA 19116. Phone is (800) 523-2930.

■ **Medic Alert International**, P.O. Box 1009, Turlock, CA 95382. Phone is (800) 344-3226. If you have special medical problems, information on your conditions can be obtained from anywhere in the world through membership in this organization.

■ **Travel Assistance International**, Worldwide Service, Inc., 1333 F St. NW, Washington, DC 20004. Phone is (800) 821-2828.

---

there. Once in your room, locate the locks, peepholes and other security devices. Make sure they work and move if they don't. Try to stay in a hotel where your room number cannot be identified from the key; where the key is not stored in a place accessible to the public in the reception area, and where the entrance and elevators are watched by staff 24 hours a day.

Unfortunately, travelers are also vulnerable to terrorism. The best way to avoid becoming a victim of terrorism is to avoid high-risk situations. No need to panic, but be realistic. I canceled a long-awaited trip to the Seychelles Islands because my departure was to occur a couple of days after the American bombing of Libya, which had been accomplished with British assistance. My flight was on British Airways, with stop-overs in London and the Middle East. All of these factors seemed too risky for a trip which could be rescheduled.

If the nightly news is reporting terrorist threats or incidents in the areas you'll be visiting or traveling through, contact the Department of State's Citizens Emergency Center (the telephone number is (202) 647-5225) for up-to-date advice on current conditions. If concern arises while you're overseas, contact the U.S. embassy or consulate.

Business executives—often considered to be prime targets—are counseled to travel as inconspicuously and anonymously as possible, not calling attention to themselves by their clothing, luggage or briefcase tags or other identifying factors.

TRAVELER'S CHECKLIST
HEALTH
....

☐ **1.** Discuss itinerary, special needs with doctor or dentist.

☐ **2.** Resolve pending medical problems such as toothache.

☐ **3.** Secure inoculations and new prescriptions.

☐ **4.** Start malaria regimen ahead of time, if recommended.

☐ **5.** Get extra supplies of prescription medications.

☐ **6.** Make sure prescriptions are properly and fully labeled.

☐ **7.** Bring along copies of prescriptions for medications and eyeglasses.

☐ **8.** Make or buy medical kit; bring extra pair of eyeglasses.

☐ **9.** Bring water purifier, canteen, if necessary.

☐ **10.** Learn how to get help in case of medical emergency.

☐ **11.** Bring along list of special medical needs, problems.

☐ **12.** Bring along insurance documents, phone numbers.

☐ **13.** Purchase extra health insurance if yours is inadequate.

Chapter Seven

HOW TO PREVENT
JET LAG

66 The spirit is indeed willing but the flesh is weak."

When this phrase was written in the Gospel of Matthew, the speediest available form of transport was probably horse or camel.

Yet it captures perfectly the frustration of sufferers of that uniquely 20th century affliction known as jet lag.

The vacationer, still clad in winter wools, WANTS to plunge from the plane into the sparkling blue Pacific and spend the day snorkeling or wind surfing.

The business executive, intent on consummating a deal, WANTS to lunch on foie gras and a fine old wine with his French counterparts and call home with the good news the same day.

But the mid-day Hawaiian sun is truly blinding; the tourist's head is buzzing; the business executive's stomach is queasy and both travelers are having trouble keeping track of time.

Vacation and business travelers alike are vulnerable to what modern science confirms is a disease of the body—not just the mind.

The popular name—jet lag—suggests that the condition is not serious. It sounds a little like, for example, "the vapors" which attacked Victorian ladies or the "liver crisis" which runs rampant among the French but seems indefinable to anyone from anywhere else in the world.

The illness surfaces in measurable physical reactions—headache, nervous stomach, fatigue and light-headedness. There is often a short-term loss of memory and a sense of detachment from the real world. While these symptoms may not seem serious, they do impair the victim's ability to function and transact business normally. There are secondary effects as well. For example, if the "mini-jet lag" experience of daylight savings time is any guide, jet lag sufferers may be more accident-prone than others. One of the top U.S. researchers in the field, Dr. Charles Ehret, reports that in statistical terms car accidents each year increase for two or three days after the time change.

Increased susceptibility to infection may be another result, given the familiar tendency of mind to affect body. The psychological symptoms of jet lag are similar to psychological depression and resemble several affective disorders. According to Ehret, "We know very well that in severe cases...this is coincidental with a decline in immune response, which opens up the body to infection." This vulnerability can be a special problem for travelers who spend time in tropical or remote areas where they may be exposed to rare or serious diseases.

The experts do not know yet if repeated exposure to long flights places frequent travelers at greater risk to jet lag and related problems than occasional ones. Ehret, a biologist at the Argonne National Laboratory near Chicago, says that the answer will be known only after more research into the workings of the "circadian rhythms" that govern eating and sleeping sleeping schedules and other body functions.

Studies of shift workers (including airline crews) required by their job responsibilities to live on atypical schedules show decreased longevity and certain health problems, but the long-term consequences are not known. It is possible, however, that intestinal functions could be affected over time. Explains Ehret: "It's a little like resetting a clock...If the system is told to go back, reset itself and start up again, this inevitably leads to some problems."

Resetting The Body Clock

Ideally, the modern Marco Polo would take an elixir or a

vaccination to prevent jet lag. But none exists.

To discover the cure, what the modern traveler requires is a good watch or clockmaker, because jet lag is essentially a malady of our internal clocks.

Through the signals known as circadian rhythms, our bodies tell us when it's time to eat or sleep or activate other body functions. Generally they instruct us to be up and about when it's light outside, and to rest when it's dark.

They are so perfectly calibrated that when we transport the body clock to a different time zone, they want to continue on the same schedule they have at home.

What you feel when you start walking on terra firma after a 10-hour flight through eight time zones may actually be a combination of jet lag, the effects of pressurization in the airplane cabin and simple fatigue.

Thus the single most important measure you can take to avoid post-travel droopiness and disorientation is to rest— before you depart, on the plane and after you arrive. For several days before you leave on a trip, suggests Ehret, creator of the anti-jet lag diet, "pad your sleep by fifteen minutes at each end, so that you go into flight not at all sleep-deprived." This recommendation, like several others which might spare us some of the impact of jet lag, obviously requires a certain amount of personal commitment and discipline.

As scientists probe and unlock the secrets of circadian rhythms they have provided travelers with additional guidance on how to minimize jet lag.

Some of their recommendations—such as following a prescribed diet for four days before and during a plane trip -- may seem prohibitively complicated or disturbing to a traveler's daily life.

Others—such as getting the right amount of sleep at the right time—may be easier to implement.

Although vacation and business travelers share the compulsion to wring the most benefit from a limited time away from home, vacationers may find it easier to take preventive steps because they have more discretion in planning their travels.

Here's what the experts recommend to limit the effects of jet lag in your next trip.

Before Departure

Schedule flight departure and arrival at times which cause the least dislocation from your normal schedule. If you're flying from New York to London, consider traveling on the daytime flight instead of leaving in the evening, losing most of a night's sleep, and arriving early in the morning British time. With the daytime flight, you'll arrive in time to eat dinner and go to sleep, and recuperation is likely to be faster.

In scheduling travel, be aware that flying east disrupts the body more than more than flying west.

". . . Traveling east, your internal body clocks suffer massive trauma. Eastbound, the sun seems to rise earlier, which means your brain is being asked to start a brand-new day six or seven hours or more earlier" than usual. "You are awake and eating on the plane, but your body temperature, hormone flow and other vital functions are still clinging to home time. Your night has been sliced in half; your new 'day' is going to be an interminable one," wrote Don Kowet in *The Jet Lag Book*.

Don't try to cover too much ground in too short a time. If you have one week for vacation, postpone the trip to a South Sea island. Otherwise, by the time you fly back, you'll barely be over the jet lag from the trip over.

The more time zones the traveler crosses, the more time is needed to overcome jet lag. Ehret says that the body normally needs one day to adjust for each time zone crossed.

Control your diet. Ehret has devised a four-day regimen designed to wean your metabolism from its normal schedule to the rhythms of your destination. It consists of alternating days of "feasting" and (relative) "fasting"; and of regulating the intake of carbohydrates , protein and caffeine for maximum benefit. Three days before departure, Ehret recommends, the traveler should "feast" on a high-protein breakfast and lunch and a high-carbohydrate dinner. The second day is a "fast" day, with intake limited to light meals such as salads, soups, fruits and juices. The day before departure is a "feast" day again, and the day of departure, a "fast day."

Don't try the diet based only on this summary description. For a wallet-sized copy of the diet which also explains how and why it works, send a stamped, self-addressed envelope to: Anti-Jet Lag Diet, OPA, Argonne National Laboratory,

---

How to Plan a Successful Trip

9700 South Cass Avenue, Argonne, IL 60439, with a stamped, self-addressed envelope. If you request it, the Laboratory will also send you a reading list on jet lag.

Avoid last-minute crises. The plane ride alone is enough of a jolt to your system. Adding the stress of an all-nighter to pack or finish a report or a frantic, last-minute dash to the airport will make your jet lag worse.

Finally, try to avoid scheduling sight-seeing or business meetings on the same day you arrive at a destination.

In Flight

Resist temptation. It's a great irony that the airlines, especially on overseas flights, compete to attract customers based on the quantity and richness of the food and drink served. The normally negative effects of consuming alcohol and rich, heavy meals—plus smoking—are exacerbated if you do it in flight. It is not your imagination: Alcohol consumption will make you drunk faster at 35,000 feet than it will on the ground.

First-class travelers face almost constant temptation. Learn to say no to the stream of canapes, oily nuts, vintage wines and after-dinner drinks. If possible, request a special, lighter meal—such as a salad—in advance. Business and first class travelers often have a more inviting selection of special meals than coach travelers, but by asking at the time you make a reservation, you may find that light meals are also available to coach class passengers. (See Chapter One, "Making Reservations: With or Without a Travel Agent," for more information on how to order special meals.)

Do not try to prevent jet lag by taking drugs such as short term sleeping pills. According to Ehret, such pills can leave you with side effects including general disorientation for a day afterwards. Available drugs, he cautions, are not sufficiently refined to ensure that they set your body clock to exactly the right schedule. In addition, studies of the effects of Halcion, one such drug, show that although it may help the traveler to sleep en route, the drug also produces the unwanted risk of amnesia for 8 to 11 hours after it is taken.

Try to sleep.

Socialize. This tip may seem contradictory to the last point. But researchers have found that "lonesome travelers" suffer greater jet lag than those who travel with a colleague or companion, or those who spend part of their trip in conversation with another passenger. Ehret recommends that on an overnight flight the time to socialize is when you wake up before arriving in the morning—not during the entire trip.

Exercise. Even a small amount of in-seat stretching and strolling around the cabin is believed to assist in minimizing jet lag.

After You Arrive

To sleep or not to sleep? Even if you've been up most of the night in the airplane, postpone sleeping at your destination until it gets dark. Don't sleep for an abnormally long time. Set the alarm clock so that your body gets the usual six or eight hours—not ten or twelve.

If you haven't done so on the plane, break the fast by eating a high-protein breakfast. Then revert to a "feast day"—meals high in carbohydrates and proteins. Most important is to adjust your dining schedule to the schedule of your destination. Avoid alcohol.

Exercise and socialize. Just as these activities are recommended while you're on the plane, they're also suggested for your hours on the ground before that first night's sleep. For example, don't dine in the solitude of your room. Go to the hotel dining room or a restaurant.

Reasonable exercise—but not more than you're accustomed to—and socializing will help you pass this somewhat foggy time faster and relax you for a good night's sleep.

Is the ultimate answer to fly the Concorde whenever possible? The 1,350-mile an hour plane will land you in Europe from the East Coast of the U.S. a couple of hours "before" your departure.

Does this mean you won't have jet lag? No, according to Ehret, but the shorter trip will lessen travel fatigue. If you keep your watch set to the clock at home, you'll be in better shape to conduct business upon arrival.

TRAVELER'S CHECKLIST
JET TRAVEL
....

☐ **1.** Look for flight options which will minimize jet lag risk.

☐ **2.** Order special, light meals for flight.

☐ **3.** Build rest and recuperation into itinerary.

☐ **4.** Bring along copy of the "Anti-Jet Lag Diet."

_____

_____

_____

_____

_____

_____

_____

_____

_____

_____

_____

_____

_____

_____

_____

Chapter Eight
ACCOMMODATING THE BUSINESS TRAVELER

Picture if you will the following: You're on a business trip. You've checked in and you've gone to your room. You pick up the phone and tell room service: "I'll have a club sandwich, iced tea and an IBM-PC."

Far-fetched? Hardly. Hotels are only one of the many commercial providers competing for the business of the business traveler. They're doing so by streamlining, gold-plating and feather-cushioning life on the road, by supplying the busy executive with a computer and many other tools of the trade that in the past he had to leave behind.

In recent years new services and gadgets, as well as discounts, clubs and "business centers" are making it increasingly possible for the business traveler to work almost from the moment he or she leaves home until they return, whether the distance traveled is 500 miles or 10,000.

The key decision today facing the business traveler is what to take along and what to leave at home. Here are some suggestions on how to answer that question for your next business trip:

■ Determine what work MUST be done while you're traveling. If you're due to get home at 10 p.m. Monday and the report must be submitted at 5 p.m. Tuesday, it's probably necessary to pack a dictating machine, portable typewriter or laptop computer so that the draft can be handed to your secretary first thing Tuesday morning.

■ Find out ahead of time what facilities are available at your hotel. When making reservations, ask whether there's a business center, what services it offers and what hours it's open. If you'll need to draft a memo on the plane, for example, you may be able to get it typed in final form when you arrive at the hotel.

■ If you'll be in one city for several days, the answer may be a temporary office where you can rent space, secure secretarial help and spend time between appointments at a desk with a telephone.

In summary, bring along as little as possible, but make sure you have the essentials.

You *Can* Take It With You

It was not long ago a clever entrepreneur introduced a "portable office," a lightweight kit containing scissors, paper clips, stapler, pen and eraser, a hole puncher, small notepad and other familiar items found on a secretary's desk. But in the last couple of years the range of office supplies and gadgets created for business travelers has leapt light years beyond the handy-dandy leather or plastic box.

Hardly a business machine exists which hasn't been, if not miniaturized, at least shrunk to fit into a briefcase or suitcase. The 5-pound sleek electronic typewriters, a new and revolutionary generation of portables when they appeared on the market a few years ago, are now complemented by increasingly smaller, more powerful laptop computers. With these svelte new machines and a diminutive printer, it's easy to carry the whole outfit in a shoulder bag.

However, travelers who plan to use their laptops in an airplane should consult the airline about it before taking off. Although a spokesman for the Federal Aviation Administration says "we have advised the airlines that the use of personal computers in flight does not constitute a problem," a spot-check revealed that some international carriers prohibit in-air use of the machine on the grounds that this interferes with radio communications systems.

You can also equip yourself with a portable copying machine, dictating equipment, long-distance beeper, fully portable cellular telephones and paging systems which—thanks to satellite technology—mean you're never really out of touch.

En Route

In some cases, it may not be worth it to pack and lug gadgets and machines. Depending on the location, business services and facilities are often available to the business traveler.

In planning your trip, think about each stage of your travel and consider how each service or facility could be effectively utilized.

Phones are commonplace in limousines and it's possible you could make good use of one during the ride to or from the airport. If so, check beforehand whether your automobile will have one. There's even a portable phone system which allows the chauffeur to answer a call, put the caller on hold, and buzz the rider in back to pick it up.

As air travel delays become a way of life, some American airports are starting to look as much like an office as a waiting room. From the tentative step of placing telephones at arm's reach at the gate and other strategic locations, creative marketers have moved on to make computers, photocopying machines, fax machines and even secretarial service convenient for the waiting or layover traveler.

One place to look for these office services and machines is in the membership clubs (e.g., TWA's Ambassador Clubs, United's Red Carpet, etc.) operated by major airlines for frequent flyers. For information on how to join, contact each airline separately. If you're flying either business or first class, in most cases you'll have access to the lounge even if you haven't paid a membership fee to join.

Another place to look is the main public areas of the airports, because AT&T and Teletrip Business Centers, an affiliate of Mutual of Omaha Insurance Co. [(800) 228-9792], are creating communications and business centers respectively that offer similar services in major airports.

Telephone service has come to Amtrak trains and to some airplanes, with wider availability predicted soon. And if someone wants to call YOU while you're in transit, they can do so by a satellite-powered long-distance paging system.

Although major business hotels have long offered to find secretarial and other business services if their guests need them, now they're putting them right into the hotel—in some cases into the rooms and in others, into a business service center. Options range from ordering a computer up to your room to assigning dictation or word processing to business center staff. In some business centers, such as the one at the Regent Hotel in Auckland, New Zealand, staff will even help you identify local business contacts and make appointments for you. Other services commonly offered are bundling up papers to mail home, translations, proofreading and beeper rentals.

In New York, the Hilton Hotel joined with Dow Jones to establish *The Wall Street Journal* Business Center in its lobby. Both guests and non-guests may rent a "work station" with personal computer, software, typewriter, office supplies, etc. by the hour or day; or engage the Center's staff to do word processing, photocopying and other tasks.

FINDING AN OFFICE ON THE ROAD

If your work requires a temporary office away from home, here are some companies that offer such facilities in U.S. and foreign cities:

■ **Headquarters Companies Network Systems**, 900 Larkspur Landing, Suite 270, Larkspur, CA 94949. Phone is (800) 227-3004.

■ **Tele-Trip Business Service Centers.** Call (800) 228-9792.

■ **World-Wide Business Centres, Inc.**, 575 Madison Ave., Suite 1006, New York, NY 10022. Phone is (212) 605-0200.

Also on site are stock market and news tickers and a reference library.

One practical source of assistance for locating all the services and facilities not readily available is a concierge, that all-purpose helpmate traditionally found in European hotels, and increasingly found in American hotels as well. Says Marie Tibor of the Washington, D.C. Convention and Visitors Association, business travelers "coming to a sophisticated city expect to have a concierge . . . who will help them meet their needs. That's the first thing I ask, personally, when I consider making a hotel reservation for a business trip."

For business travelers who need meeting space or want the appearance of an established office in far-flung places, it's becoming easier to located furnished, staffed office space both near airports and in the center of town a list of companies offering these facilities. (See box.)

How to Find the Business Essentials

Most major business hotel chains have toll-free phone numbers from which you can get information about their services. Your travel agent should also be able to secure some of this information from a computer search. By 1988, among those which offer business services and facilities at many of their hotels both in the U.S. and abroad are Hilton, Hyatt International, Inter-Continental, Radisson, Regent, Sheraton, Stouffer and Westin.

In many cases, these and other hotels configure some guest rooms on "executive" floors on which the business traveler will find a receptionist, a conference room or lounge, newspapers outside the door in the morning and other special facilities and services.

For information on business service facilities at airport clubs, call the airlines or your frequent flyer club. Mutual of Omaha's Tele-Trip Centers offer small suites with a desk and phones; as well as secretarial service, a notary and use of various business machines.

But Don't Overdo It

As the services and gadgets for business travelers proliferate, psychologists are raising questions about whether they really benefit the already stressed executive, or whether they just make him or her a candidate for a heart attack at an earlier age.

Dr. Daniel L. Araoz, a psychologist from Long Island who specializes in working with business executives, cautions travelers not to work all of the time they're on the road. "We are bombarded by all of these advances," he observes. If you insist on keeping the laptop or the telephone only an arm's length away while on the road, he suggests, make sure to structure your week or even better, your day, to include "pockets of personal time" to relieve tension and reflect on your work.

TRAVELER'S CHECKLIST
BUSINESS TRIPS

● ●

☐ **1.** Decide what hardware to take along—computer, dictaphone, etc.

☐ **2.** Check restrictions on carry-ons, use of laptop computer in flight.

☐ **3.** Register hardware with U.S. Customs and/or secure carnet.

☐ **4.** Secure permits for entry of computer, etc. into foreign countries.

☐ **5.** Identify business facilities and services available at airports and hotels.

☐ **6.** Does hotel have special floor or section for business travelers?

☐ **7.** Arrange to communicate with office by phone, fax, etc.

_____

_____

_____

_____

_____

_____

_____

_____

How to Plan a Successful Trip

Chapter Nine

WHEN A FAMILY
TRAVELS

As summer or holiday season approaches, so does the question of how to observe the annual ritual known as The Family Vacation.

American as apple pie and as old as the automobile, the ritual has been defined historically as "piling into the family car." The vacation consisted not only of GOING somewhere, but also of enjoying The Process of Getting There.

Although an estimated 80 percent of family vacations still involve some time in the car, social and demographic trends are propelling many families to seek—and find—new ways to relax together and new, hospitable environments in which to do it.

More than 60 percent of mothers of school-aged children work outside the home. More children than ever grow up in families where both parents work, or live with only one parent. Grandparents reside hundreds or even thousands of miles from their grandchildren. Thus the family vacation has become one of the few times when parents, children and sometimes grandparents can enjoy quality time together.

Packing the family into the car and heading for Yellowstone Park with a tent remains an attractive, economically viable option for millions of American families.

But many families are willing and able to exceed the geographical and financial limits of a campground or nearby

---

beach or lakeside cottage or even rent a villa abroad or fly across the country to spend a week at a dude ranch. No frontier seems too distant or too exotic to conquer. Some children return to "show and tell" after summer vacation with souvenirs of an African safari, a week in Paris or snorkeling on Australia's Great Barrier Reef.

Articles on "how to travel with your family" seem to appear as often as articles how to get away from the kids (or the in-laws). And hotels, resorts and airlines compete for the family trade with a growing range of enticements ranging from children's menus and family room rates to airport play areas to minimize the stress of waiting for flights. Some of these services also make it possible for high-powered working parents to take their children—especially preschoolers—along on business trips.

Where to Go With the Children

But finding the perfect family vacation spot is not always easy.

Dorothy Jordon is the founder of the "Travel With Your Children" (TWYCH) resource center in New York. Through a newsletter and books, the Center counsels parents on how to plan family vacations and suggests specific destinations and hotels which welcome families.

Jordon recommends that families discuss together what type of vacation would appeal to everyone. When young children are involved, consider their needs first, she suggests.

The difficulties of finding the right spot are illustrated by this experience of one family, with two children under ten years old, when they checked into a highly recommended "family resort" in a Western state.

"The hot tubs and sauna were out of bounds to children; the children were asked to 'keep quiet' in the so-called 5-star dining room at dinner time; and they were asked to stay out of the library at dinner time because it was near the dining room.

"It looked like a family resort," recalls the children's mother, Maxine Freund of Washington, D.C., "but they didn't want kids to act like kids."

On another, more satisfying vacation they stayed in a

lodge which provided activities for the whole family. "One night they had a cookout. The kids ate first, hot dogs from the grill. Then the children went on a hayride while the adults ate their steak. When they came back, we all learned to square dance together," she recalls.

For several years Freund has made an avocation of seeking appropriate family vacation spots, first by reading general guidebooks, then by focusing on interesting destinations.

But to ensure that such establishments really encourage family trade rather than just tolerate it, she's learned to speak to proprietors and managers of hotels and resorts as well as to people who have actually been there before making a reservation.

The Freund family prefers to have a base to which they can return for several nights in a row, avoiding packing, repacking and long car trips.

What exactly does Freund look for in a vacation destination?

■ The precise location is less important than what the family can do there. She looks for active physical activities—horseback riding, swimming, skiing, etc.—to keep young bodies active and challenged;

■ Proximity to airport, train or short car ride, to avoid long, tiring car trips;

■ Presence of other children;

■ A welcoming, understanding attitude toward children.

Jordon also suggests destinations which have educational value for the children. "As kids get older, it gets to be more fun," she says. "If your children have read Mark Twain, take a steamship up the Mississippi. Try to relate the trip to things which are happening in your children's lives—at school, on television, etc."

Facilities and Services

Once the destination has been identified, the next step is to make sure that the space and the services meet the family's requirements.

"Space is very important," emphasizes Jordon. "Some parents take kids on a vacation from a big house, cramp themselves into a small hotel room . . . and then wonder why they're not having a good time. Often renting a suite or a villa or exchanging a house with another family provides more space and is more economical."

Two major considerations prevail. One is whether the destination is physically set up to accommodate families comfortably; the other is the availability of services which will free all family members from routine tasks such as laundry and cooking.

Here are suggestions for a family of four:

■ Two adjoining (not just side by side) bedrooms, perhaps a one-bedroom suite which makes up into two bedrooms. Thus parents and children each have their privacy, but they are accessible to each other in a matter of seconds;

■ A place where the family can eat breakfast other than in a communal dining room, and to which they can return at the end of the day to play games or relax as a family;

■ Daily housekeeping and laundry service.

Depending on the age of the children, you may want to add these to your list:

■ Cribs, cots and high chairs;

■ Child care or babysitting service, perhaps during the day as well as at night;

■ A refrigerator in the room, for snacks and milk for babies;

■ Special room rates—e.g., no charge for a child who sleeps in the parents' room.

Three-Generation Vacations

A family vacation can also involve three generations, but with an age span of 50 or 60 years, the needs are bound to be more complicated.

Although every family is different, experts on travel by senior citizens caution that stereotypes may be misleading and may result in underestimating the stamina and appetite of the elderly for travel. "Older people feel younger than their physical years," according to a study of their travel habits by the American Association of Retired Persons (AARP). "Research indicates that lifestyles are changing, that older Americans are enjoying better health longer," concluded the AARP study. According to the research, senior citizens actually journey further away and stay away longer than other travelers. For example, the average length of a journey by a person over 65 years old was found to be more than 2,000 miles, triple the average distance covered by other travelers.

But even vigorous grandparents may require ramps, safety bars in the bathroom and other special physical features as well as flexible space which provides for some time with the children and some time away from them.

As in the case of a parent-child holiday, when grandparents are to be included, they should be part of the family planning conclave so that they are assured that the plans will accommodate their level of physical stamina.

Some families who have tried the multi-generational approach caution that coping with changes in physical environment, schedule and routine for three generations at once can be trying. It's important to consider all of these factors before committing to a particular location.

For example, children and grandparents may have different ideas about how long to stay at the beach. If the kids want to spend the whole day and the grandparents want to stay an hour or two, don't choose a hotel or apartment that's an hour's drive from the beach.

Jordon offers a model of a successful three-generation trip taken by her family: "I rented a 4-bedroom apartment at a Puerto Rico resort for my parents, my two children, my sister's two children and myself," she recalls. "My parents are avid golfers and had a chance to play. They loved spending time with the kids. My older nephews played for hours with the younger kids, and part of the time we got babysitters from the resort." Another possible solution, she suggested, is to travel together on a cruise ship which provides separate quarters for different generations but lots of opportunity to spend time together.

Getting There

By plane: Before you book your family vacation, ask the airlines if they have special family rates and/or services or facilities for children. With airport delays, keeping children occupied and keeping track of them and their belongings is a bigger problem than in the past. Members of frequent flyer clubs or travelers who can afford business or first class at least have access to airport lounges with comfortable seats, free snacks and beverages, and a self-contained space in which youngsters can play more safely than in the general waiting lounges.

Some airports offer supervised or unsupervised play areas for children regardless of which class they are flying. "Kidsport," at New York's LaGuardia and Pittsburgh's International airports, is furnished with toys and equipment such as a slide. Airlines including SAS at the Copenhagen airport and Australian Airlines at the Brisbane, Australia facility offer similar centers.

If a child must travel alone on a plane, ask the airline what services it offers for unaccompanied minors. These may range from providing an escort and supervision during lay-overs to resolving problems resulting from delays or cancellations. (In some cases, unaccompanied minors who require an escort are charged an adult fare or something more than the normal fare for children.) Some airlines, such as TWA, United and British Caledonian, have special rooms in some airports where these young travelers can play games, read and get something to eat or drink between flights.

Family members of all ages can benefit from learning the layout and facilities of airports before arriving. How long a walk is it from the arrival gate of one airline to the gate for your connecting flight on another airline? How can you arrange for a cart, wheelchair or other assistance for children or grandparents who may not be able to cover the distance on foot? Are there luggage carts to transport your carry-ons from gate to gate or to move your luggage from the baggage claim to ground transportation? If not, consider bringing your own.

Some of this information can be gleaned from resources listed in the appendix or from guidebooks to specific destinations. According to Dorothy Jordon, however, there is no comprehensive guide to facilities and services for children and families traveling by air. Thus you should make a point of asking those questions when you book a plane trip, or of having your travel agent request the information for you.

By Train: Families can view a train trip as a way to get somewhere or as an end in itself. If you're going to be on the train overnight, ask Amtrak for the specifications for sleeping cars. In the category known as "family bedroom," each car has berths for both children and adults. Amtrak can also give you specifications on the room for luggage storage in each type of sleeping accommodation. It is also possible to check luggage

Families planning to travel on trains overseas—like airline passengers—will have to ask ahead of time or depend on general railway guides for information about facilities and services for families.

By Car: If the vehicle is your family car or one rented from a major U.S. company, you can probably count on encountering seat belts in the back seat and can use your own or acquire another car seat, if necessary. AAA and Mobil Travel guides offer considerable detail about services on the road for families traveling by car.

The number one caution for families planning a car trip is to avoid trying to cover too much ground. Plan an itinerary which will offer interesting side trips and breaks so that the family is not subjected to claustrophobic, nerve-fraying stretches in the car. AAA members can get a detailed intinerary and planning assistance by requesting a "Triptik."

By Bus: The danger of overdoing the travel time and underdoing the vacation time also applies to bus trips, whether by scheduled service or with a tour group. Don't accept what the tour brochure says at face value.

If you can talk to another family who's taken the tour you're interested in, the feedback on their experience is likely to be the most useful information.

Also, do your own research—or ask your travel agent to help—on the details of the itinerary. Consult a map, check the distances, see if the times are realistic. Are the visits and accommodations on the tour really appropriate for your toddler or your 70-year-old mother? What exactly are the accommodations?

Can your family make the one-mile hike from the road to the waterfall? Or to the top of the mountain? Will some family members be forced into a schedule which is too tiring? Is there enough free time for weary travelers to collapse and take a nap, or for restless youngsters to stretch their legs and get rid of pent-up energy? If you're using a travel agent, also ask his or her help in answering these questions before signing on the dotted line.

Packing

For any trip, give careful thought to the special needs of your children while traveling. Plan far enough ahead to ensure that you have time before you leave to organize and, if necessary, to buy the essentials—from diapers to favorite snacks for the car. And for every child who's old enough, consider purchasing a small backpack which holds both the essential change of clothes and toys and books or other tools for whiling away travel time—plus the most beloved stuffed animal or blanket. If you're looking for new ideas on how to keep traveling children occupied, the November 1987 issue of the TWYCH newsletter cited below contains an article on "Travel Toys Kids Like Best."

Advance Planning

1. Have you discussed the itinerary and length of the trip with all the participants?

2. If more than one family will be paying expenses, have you agreed on what you can afford to spend?

3. Do you know anyone who has taken a similar trip with the family? What was their experience? Did the hotel really welcome children? Were the train compartments comfortable enough for sleeping?

4. Do you know exactly what services and facilities are

offered? Does the resort/cruise ship/national park offer all the basics your family needs for a successful trip? Does your hotel room have a refrigerator where you can store milk and snacks?

5. If you're traveling by plane, have you checked on how to get a wheelchair for grandmother? Whether you'll find luggage carts at the airport?

6. If children are traveling alone, do you know how they can get assistance if their flight is delayed? If they become ill while on the train?

7. For car trips or tours, have you studied the itinerary to make sure it's appropriate for your family? Have you looked at a map so you know how many hours a day you'll be in the car or bus?

8. Have you made a packing list? Have you decided which luggage to take, and which family member will be responsible for carrying which pieces? Is there time to purchase supplies of special items such as toys and diapers before you go?

TRAVELER'S CHECKLIST
FAMILY TRIPS

· ·

- [ ] **1.** Build time for making travel connections and for rest into itinerary.

- [ ] **2.** Get new passports or visas for all family members.

- [ ] **3.** For air travel: Arrange for special meals, seats, wheel chair, etc.

- [ ] **4.** For child traveling alone: Arrange for supervision and emergency help.

- [ ] **5.** Equip each child with identification.

- [ ] **6.** Make sure all items on list have been packed.

_____

_____

_____

_____

_____

_____

_____

_____

_____

_____

_____

Chapter Ten

YOUR RIGHTS AS A TRAVEL CONSUMER

I wanted the most economical round trip airfare from London to Washington. But on this trip, I knew it was likely that the date of my return to the U.S. would change while I was in Europe.

"Please find the best fare you can," I told the travel agent. "But I'm willing to pay a little more to make sure I can change the return flight without incurring a large penalty." I repeated my instructions several times.

"If you have to change the date of return," she told me when I picked up the ticket, "it will cost you only fifty dollars."

Nearly two months later I was ensconced in a manor house at a conference in the English countryside. Not feeling well, I wanted to go home sooner than anticipated, and needed to change the date of my flight. Both the travel agent in the tiny nearby town and the airline reservations office with which I talked by phone in London insisted that my ticket could not be changed—that the only way to get home sooner was to buy a regular fare one-way ticket. The cost—nearly $600—was about the same as my original round trip "bargain."

There seemed to be no recourse, so I charged the new ticket to a credit card and flew home to begin to press my claim for reimbursement. Knowing this could be a long fight, I made two strategy decisions:

■ To start with the person who had sold me the airline ticket but, if necessary, to quickly escalate my demands to the top level of both the travel agency and the airline;

■ To demand reimbursement of the cost of the entire new ticket, plus cost of the return portion of the original ticket which I was unable to use to return to the U.S. (I did not expect to be reimbursed for the old. As an experienced bargainer, I assumed that it would be necessary to request more so that the final compromise would result in what I thought I deserved.)

My campaign for satisfaction was waged on two fronts for several weeks. Even with the ticket in hand, the travel agency and the airline could not agree on the conditions on the ticket I'd been sold. The agency said I could have used it for the return, but the airline said I could not have. What was clear to me was that I had not received the ticket I'd requested, and that this was not my fault.

The airline "generously" offered to placate me by letting me use the remaining one-way ticket from London to Washington (which had theoretically expired) any time before the end of the year. But this would have required me to buy another return ticket—an expensive proposition—and I didn't even WANT to go back to London so soon.

Several weeks later, after numerous phone calls, letters and a personal visit to the head of the airline's local ticket office, someone finally got tired of listening to me. The airline and the agency agreed to accept joint responsibility for the error, and each reimbursed me for half of the cost of the new ticket.

Exhausted and frustrated by the process, I crossed the travel agency off my list and vowed to try to avoid flying on that airline again.

The traveler encounters all too many of these types of experiences. We all hope for the perfect trip, and actually receiving what we thought we bought—whether it's an airline flight, a hotel, or a tour package—is a critical part of achieving this perfection.

Yet it seems harder all the time. Airline deregulation has narrowed our choice of carriers and flights to many destinations. Deciding on a destination or hotel or itinerary or whether to rent a car seems to get more complicated. Special packages and discounts exist one day and disappear the next. The fine print seems unintelligible. Even the experts have trouble finding what's current in a computer, and all of these factors can cause honest mistakes and much confusion.

As if this weren't enough, the travel consumer faces the problem of avoiding not just honest mistakes, but the possibility of entrapment by organized racketeers promoting travel "scams"—seemingly irresistible offers of free or bargain travel which exist only to line the pockets of the criminals who make off with the prospective traveler's money and provide no trip.

None of these problems or frustrations are a product of our imaginations. The Deputy Attorney General of the State of California reported that in one month of (February) 1987 alone, her office received 265 complaints about travel scams. The Council of Better Business Bureaus reports that for 1986, its affiliates received more than 57,000 requests for information about travel agencies, and some 5,300 complaints from consumers. Although these are not necessarily travel-related, the Council also receives substantial numbers of complaints about credit cards and insurance companies. And in 1987 the U.S. Department of Transportation (DOT) received nearly 45,000 complaints about airline service—compared with 12,752 the year before.

There are few laws to protect consumers against mistakes or even scams in the travel industry. Perhaps if there were more, our complaints to consumer agencies would bring more satisfaction.

Federal Laws

On the federal level, the most explicit consumer protections for travelers apply to airline transportation. DOT's pamphlet "Fly-Rights" summarizes your rights as an airline traveler. They include your right to receive up to $1,250 in reimbursement for luggage lost or damaged while in the care of a domestic airline; and your right to a seat in the non-smoking section of the plane as long as you're not traveling on stand-by and don't arrive late. In addition, airlines are required to prohibit all smoking on flights of less than two hours. Passengers who transgress are subject to $1,000 in civil penalties. (Although your actual legal rights as an airline passenger are very limited, the "Fly-Rights" pamphlet does a good job of explaining how you might be most effective in avoiding or resolving disputes with airlines on such issues as overbooking and refunds. It's available from the Office of the Secretary of Transportation, 400 Seventh St. SW, Washington, DC 20590.)

There is some hope that air passengers' rights will be augmented by proposed legislation (pending in Congress in 1988) resulting from the crescendo of consumer frustration over air travel delays and cancellations. The Airline Passengers of America, an organization which proclaimed its own "Bill of Rights" for passengers, joined other consumer groups in lobbying Congress to require airlines to provide consumers with information on their performance and to compensate passengers who are bumped due to overbooking, who are left holding unusable tickets due to an airline bankruptcy or whose baggage is lost.

Also on the national level, the Federal Trade Commission has authority to take legal action against perpetrators of "unfair and deceptive" practices, and has become involved in a national effort to inform consumers about travel scams sponsored by vacation clubs. However, the agency does not represent individual consumers. If you register a complaint against, for example, a hotel or car rental chain, the FTC will only become involved if it appears that a large number of consumers are affected.

Neither the data on travel frauds nor the legislative activity tells the whole story of the importance of having a successful travel experience. Travel plays a special psychological role in our lives. If a mix-up or extra expense ruins a vacation, we feel doubly cheated because that's a prescribed time for enjoyment which we'll never get back. If the delay or mix-up occurs on a business trip, it can mean loss of time which is often equivalent to a loss of money, or even loss of a deal.

So if the best-laid plans and promises don't work out, what can the traveler do to get satisfaction?

Preventive Strategies

Ask questions before you buy. Says the American Society of Travel Agents (ASTA) in a useful pamphlet, "Avoiding Travel Problems": "In general, all companies promoting travel should be willing to fully disclose all relevant details about the offer they're making."

You and your travel agent may use the "Air Travel Consumer Report," published monthly by the DOT, to check the delay and cancellation records of domestic airlines, as well as to see which ones have the largest number of reports of lost, mishandled or damaged baggage. In cases where you do have a choice of flights, this information might assist in choosing one. Your travel agent should have this information in the computer. But if you want to order the report, write the DOT Office of Consumer Affairs, 400 Seventh Street NW, Room 1045, Washington, DC 20590.

Learn about the conditions attached to your purchase.

Airline Tickets:

When purchasing an airline ticket, be aware that any fare which is not the "normal" or "regular" one is likely to be subject to requirements and penalties. Here are some of the common ones to ask about:

■ Must the ticket be used only on certain days of the week—e.g., Monday through Thursday?

■ Must the ticket be used within a certain time period? Will it expire two months from now whether you use it or not?

■ Are there penalties for cancellation or changes? One reason I ultimately won my battle over the London ticket was that I had stated my preference clearly to the travel agent and only the most thick-skinned liar could have denied it later. If you know that your two-week vacation absolutely cannot be extended a day or two, then the penalty for changing the date won't be an issue. But if your return date is flexible or you don't know how long your business will take, don't get locked into these types of restrictions.

- Delays and other defaults: If the flight is canceled or delayed, what will the airline do to assist you to travel as planned? If you're stranded, will they offer a free hotel room and meals?

Hotel and Tours:

Reservations for hotels and tour packages may also be encumbered by restrictions and penalties.

Does your hotel reservation require a deposit or a guarantee? What happens if you must cancel at the last minute? Often hotels will only hold a reserved room until a certain time, such as 9 p.m. Ask if they'll hold it later if you're delayed and call to say that you're on the way.

In some cases, overbooked hotels give away your room even if it is pre-paid, and in the worst case they may not help you find another place to sleep.

When booking a tour package, ask for the name of your hotel as well as a description of it. This will enable you to check the location and facilities with an independent source such as a guidebook or to even call yourself and ask about the facilities.

Car Rentals:

Renting cars also raises a series of thorny questions for the consumer. Before signing on the dotted line of a contract, review all of the charges. If you're renting from a major company, it's easy for the agent to ask the computer to run off a tentative bill which itemizes the anticipated charges. The "drop-off charge," imposed for returning the car in a different city or town from the one where you rent it, is one fee that often comes as a surprise at the end of a trip.

Cars are generally rented by the 24-hour period but charges for keeping the car a few hours longer can vary considerably. If you keep the car for an additional three hours, will you be charged an hourly rate or will you have to pay for another day?

Before driving off, find out what to do in case of an accident or breakdown. I learned this the hard way on a trip to Canada when my traveling companion and I had to buy a new tire for a rental car. The cost was supposed to be covered by the rental company, which had a toll-free number. However, we had rented the car in the U.S. and were stranded in a tiny village in Nova Scotia where the toll-free number didn't work. After numerous inquiries through the phone operators and local tire store, we still hadn't located anyone from the car rental company to take responsibility for accepting the cost of the tire. My friend put the charge on a credit card and settled it at the end of the trip when he returned the car.

All-Purpose Tips:

Here are some tips to keep in mind when making any kind of travel arrangements—for flights, hotels, tours or cars:

■ If you don't get satisfactory answers to your questions, don't make a financial commitment. Take your business elsewhere.

■ Create a paper trail. Get documents for all your travel arrangements, and keep copies for future reference. Receipts, notes of conversations, etc. may be not just useful but essential if you have to make a fight later.

■ Know your rights before you make a commitment.

■ Choose your method of payment carefully.

In the case of my London ticket, I avoided paying out the cost of the new ticket because it was charged to an American Express card. Some but not all credit card companies allow you to postpone payment of a charge as long as you have an unresolved dispute with the hotel, airline or other company which is charging you. Before withholding payment, however, check with your credit card company about the procedure to be followed. In every case back up your action by enclosing a letter with your monthly payment which explains why you are withholding a particular charge.

Airline tickets can present special problems if they are charged to a credit card. Even if you don't use the ticket, you are likely to be billed for it. In such cases you'll have to go through the process of having the account credited. DOT points out in "Fly-Rights" that if you change your flight after you have charged it, the ticket agent may want to credit the amount of the old tickets and issue another set with a second charge to your account. You may want to insist that the value of your old tickets be applied to the new ones, with the difference in price charged or credited to your account. If you're not using a credit card, pay with a check so that you have an official record of the transaction.

Choosing a Remedy

What can you do when prevention fails? Start by deciding what you want. Some options:

Money: e.g., the cost of the extra ticket you had to buy.

Replacement in kind: Did your vacation tour promise a room in a 5-star hotel but deliver a 2-star room instead? Maybe your demand should be to receive the same number of nights in a 5-star hotel, or a refund of the difference in the room rate between the 5-star and the 2-star hotels.

Facilities and arrangements: Did you get stuck in a strange city overnight, miss your connecting flight and lose your hotel room at the ultimate destination? Perhaps you need to demand a new airline ticket and the cost of the meals and hotel required to recoup and do your business.

Damages: Don't get your hopes up, advises a lawyer at Ralph Nader's Aviation Consumer Action Project. Airlines customarily say that they do not guarantee their schedules and thus you won't have a legal leg to stand on if you miss a meeting or a vacation because your flight is delayed or canceled. Only if an airline clerk errs and guarantees a departure or arrival time would the consumer have grounds to seek damages. Other experts say that for the most common travel complaints—such as being assigned an inferior hotel room or not receiving all the promised elements of a tour—your best hope is to pursue the types of remedies suggested above.

How to Get What You Want—By Yourself

Start with a direct personal contact with the individual or agency which goofed or misled you. If the response is encouraging, follow up immediately with a letter stating the problem clearly and outlining what you expect to be done about it. Enclose copies—not originals—of relevant documents. Keep the originals until such time as you may be required by a court or other official proceeding to produce them.

Don't waste too much time waiting for replies. Delay is the time-honored method of dealing with frustrated consumers. If there's no follow-up within a week, call back.

If functionaries seem recalcitrant, escalate to the top. Lower-level employees who caused the error may assume you'll get tired of fighting and give up in the hope that their work may not be questioned.

If you're dealing with an airline or other large company, be sure to initiate the contact by writing a letter. In this case, I suggest writing to the president. You may not end up talking to the president, but letters sent to that office are likely to receive some attention when they're forwarded to an appropriate subordinate.

If the problem is with a local travel agency, a phone call to the manager may be sufficient to get the case moving. Always follow up with a letter, though.

The "Consumer's Resource Handbook" is a free document which may help you plan your strategy and decide which public or private agency to approach for assistance. It contains the names and addresses of consumer affairs officials of major corporations (including airlines and car rental companies) as well of state and local government agencies, trade associations and professional groups which may be able to help you. You can order a copy of the handbook—

which was compiled jointly by U.S. government agencies and the Council of Better Business Bureaus—from the Consumer Information Center, Pueblo, CO 81009.

Third-Party Assistance

If all other strategies have failed, consider enlisting the help of a third party. This escalation will require more time and energy, and you'll have to decide whether the harm done to you—and the potential compensation—are sufficient to justify it.

Here are some places you might seek help and the type of assistance you can receive from them:

American Society of Travel Agents (ASTA): This organization has a code of ethics and its ultimate sanction is to expel members who do not live up to the code. If you have a dispute with one of ASTA's member agencies (about half of the U.S. total), you may request the national organization to help resolve it. "Avoiding Travel Problems," a free ASTA pamphlet, contains a list of the organization's "principles of professional conduct and ethics" and outlines the procedure for seeking assistance through the national group. If the dispute can't be resolved through ASTA, you may be referred to government agencies, small claims court or other possible means of recourse.

Better Business Bureau (BBB): Your local branch will arrange a mediation process if it is seen as an appropriate way to resolve your dispute with a travel-related organization. BBB also offers a free third-party arbitration service but because it's voluntary there is no way an aggrieved consumer can force the accused agency or company to participate. If it turns out that the consumer's dispute is really with a national company headquartered in another jurisdiction, such as an airline, it might be necessary to incur costs to participate in arbitration by conference call or traveling out of town. For details on how to get help from BBB, write for the organization's booklet entitled "Arbitration— A National Program of Dispute Resolution," request Publication No. 24-165 from the Council of Better Business Bureaus, 1515 Wilson Boulevard, Arlington, VA 22209.

Local or state consumer affairs agencies: Many states, cities and counties have consumer affairs offices which will assist you in pursuing a complaint against a business in their jurisdiction. Consumer protection laws vary from one jurisdiction to another, so your ability to pursue satisfaction through legal channels may depend on where you live.

Federal agencies: You can file a complaint about airline service by calling the Department of Transportation's consumer affairs bureau at (202) 366-2220 between 8:30 a.m. and 5 p.m. Eastern Time. A counselor will suggest how you can resolve your complaint through local or state or private channels. If you have exhausted these channels, the Department may help you by calling the airline and trying to negotiate directly on your behalf. This office handled more than 44,000 complaints in 1987 and only has five full-time staff persons, so don't expect your request to be expedited.

To alert federal authorities to an unfair or deceptive practice such as a travel scam, write to the Public Reference Bureau, Room 130, Federal Trade Commission, Washington, DC 20580. But remember that the agency only acts on complaints which affect a group of consumers so you will not get assistance in resolving your own particular problem.

Members of Congress: If you're not certain your complaint falls under federal law, write to or call the local office of your U.S. Representative or Senator. Each office has a caseworker whose job it is to assist constituents with these types of problems.

News media: If you feel your problem may affect other consumers and other methods are not working, try contacting a local newspaper or broadcast "consumer hotline." Public disclosure can often be more effective than going to court.

To summarize, your legal rights as a consumer of travel services are relatively limited. The remedies open to you in many cases cannot possibly compensate for the loss of time, money or peace of mind occasioned by delays, or failure to receive the services promised by the vendors.

For those who believe that in travel, "the trip is the thing," another message is warranted: Prevention can, and often does, work. What could determine the success of your next journey is not so much which beach you chose to lie on or which business contact you targeted for the next deal—but whether you put aside a few minutes or an hour ahead of time to engage, not in fantasies, but in planning.

In other words: anticipate the unexpected.

TRAVELER'S CHECKLIST
CONSUMER PROTECTION
••••••••••••••••••••••••••••••••••••

☐ **1.** Check reputation of travel business with consumer officials or Better Business Bureau.

☐ **2.** Before booking, check airline records on delays, cancellations, baggage handling.

☐ **3.** Learn about penalties for cancellations or reservation changes.

☐ **4.** Check travel documents for accuracy before paying for them.

☐ **5.** Secure written confirmation for all travel arrangements.

☐ **6.** Leave copy of vouchers, etc. at home and give one to traveling companion.

☐ **7.** When paying for reservations, leave a paper trail.

☐ **8.** Request receipts and file them.

_____

_____

_____

_____

_____

_____

APPENDIX

Contents:

TEN TRAVEL DISASTERS:
How to Avoid—or at Least Minimize—Them

1. Missing Your Plane (Or Train or Bus)

Before You Go:

■ Make sure time and destination on ticket are accurate;

■ Find out if you will be crossing any time zones. Any seasonal changes due? Does your schedule take these into account?

■ Obtain transportation schedules to carry with you—so that you're able to ascertain quickly the next departure if you've missed a flight, train or bus. Alternatively, jot down the information in wallet or similar place next to scheduled departures.

While Traveling:

■ Reconfirm airline reservations according to instructions (usually 72 hours ahead). At the same time, make sure you have accurate information on time and place of departure (especially if there is more than one airport or station in the area).

■ Inform yourself about the availability of transportation

to stations and airports; give yourself plenty of time to get there.

■ Before leaving for an airport or station, call to see if flight or train is on time (especially if there may be weather problems).

2. Losing Luggage

Before you go:

■ Bring along sturdy luggage, which can be locked.

■ Pack a carry-on bag with essentials that would enable you to function even if checked luggage is lost.

■ Label all your bags, inside and out.

While Traveling:

■ Make sure ticket agents have tagged your luggage for the proper destination; keep your eye on it until you're sure it has been sent from the baggage counter to the plane or train.

■ If making a connection in a busy airport, consider — if time allows—checking your luggage only to the intermediate destination, then picking it up and re-checking it for second flight.

3. Trouble at the Border—On the Way In or On the Way Out

Before you go:

■ Allow yourself several weeks to obtain passports, visas and any other documents required for international travel.

■ If you're planning to visit a troubled area or a country

---

with which the United States has unfriendly relations, arrange to enter through a major airport or station rather than an isolated checkpoint.

■ Investigate customs requirements of countries you are planning to visit.

While traveling:

■ If visiting a troubled area keep up with the news; don't take unnecessary risks.

■ Always know how to reach the closest U.S. embassy or consulate.

■ Do not travel with illicit drugs, firearms or other items that are either illegal or likely to cause concern to customs officials.

4. Sickness, Injuries and Other Medical Emergencies

Before You Go:

■ Attend to all medical and dental problems before you leave. Consider having a check-up if it has been some time since your last.

■ Inform yourself about potential health risks at your destination and prepare for them with inoculations, a malaria regimen or other appropriate measures.

■ Pack adequate supplies of prescriptions and other medications you may require; keep in your hand luggage.

■ Bring along a small first aid kit.

■ If you have chronic problems and are concerned about a possible emergency, consider taking out supplementary health or emergency evacuation insurance and/or joining an organization that can help you in these cases. (See Chapter Six, "Your Health and Safety.")

While Traveling:

■ If food and water pose a health risk, don't take chances by consuming raw food, ice or unboiled or non-carbonated beverages.

■ Try to get adequate rest so that your resistance is not sapped by the extra rigors of travel.

■ In case of serious illness or death of a traveling companion overseas, contact the U.S. embassy or nearest consulate for guidance on how to find a doctor or appropriate authorities.

5. Unpleasant Weather

Before you go:

■ Consult an atlas or guidebook for details on high and low temperatures and precipitation at your destination during the time of year you'll be visiting. Check your local newspaper's weather page; many give previous day's high and low temperatures for the world's major cities. Keep in mind that promotional brochures don't always provide a full and an accurate picture of a country or area's weather conditions.

■ Based on what you learn about weather patterns, pack umbrella, wool socks or other gear you might need.

While Traveling:

■ In destinations with severe or erratic weather, keep up with forecasts and avoid outings that could be affected by difficult conditions. In scheduling outdoor excursions in which pre- or partial payment is required ascertain what happens in the event of bad weather.

6. Crime

Before you go:

■ Learn what you can about crime risks at your destination. Are tourists a particular target of pickpockets, muggers and other criminals? Seek information from your travel agent, business colleagues and others who have visited areas where you are headed. Many crimes can be avoided if you simply know what to look for.

■ Decide how you are going to carry your money and other valuables. If necessary, acquire a money belt or similar device.

■ Before booking a hotel, make sure it's in a neighborhood where you'll feel safe.

While Traveling:

■ Be observant in your new surroundings. If you're not comfortable in a neighborhood, don't walk around alone.

■ If you have serious questions about your safety in a particular location, ask the U.S. embassy or consulate for advice.

■ Carry with you the emergency information card found at the back of this book; give a copy to a traveling companion.

■ Never carry on your person more money, valuables, documents or credit cards than you need.

■ If you're staying in a reliable hotel, leave your valuables in the safe.

7. Running Out of Money

Before You Go:

■ Make a realistic estimate of how much money you will need until you return home.

- If traveling overseas, consider bringing with you a small amount of currency to cover taxicabs and other essentials when you first arrive. Foreign currency exchange centers can be found in many American cities and at international airports.

- Bring along with you at least two different instruments for securing money, such as travelers checks and a credit card. Where one doesn't work, the other might.

- Bring along a list of sources for emergency cash. (See Chapter Five, "Money Matters.")

While Traveling:

- Do not carry large quantities of cash.

- Keep informed about regular bank schedules and bank holidays. These can differ drastically from country to country and even within the United States.

8. Choosing the Wrong Travel Companion

Before you go:

- Give some thought to your own travel habits before choosing a companion or companions. Do you like simple accommodations or expensive ones? Do you enjoy museums but hate hiking? What is your travel pace? What are the preferences of prospective companions?

- Talk frankly with your prospective fellow travelers, both about itinerary and what you'd expect of each other on a daily basis.

- Don't be afraid to travel alone. Unless your destination is exceedingly "foreign" and possibly dangerous, your travels can be enriched by encounters and opportunities that arise because you are alone.

- Before signing up for a tour, learn as much as possible about the type of people who are likely to participate and how the itinerary is structured. As a precaution, select a tour with an itinerary that provides some opportunity to get away from the group occasionally.

While Traveling:

■ Talk out your differences and problems with your companion, rather than allowing them to build into tensions and overwhelming proportions.

■ To avoid the pressure of seeing too much of each other, arrange your schedule to provide some time alone, doing what each of you really wants to do.

9. Bad Bookings

Before you go:

■ Read all the fine print before you commit to an air fare, charter, tour or hotel. Make sure you know exactly what services and facilities are included and how much everything is to cost.

■ Check your travel arrangements with an independent source, someone such as a friend who has made the same trip or an up-to-date, reliable guidebook that offers critiques of facilities and services.

■ Have your travel agent or the providers supply you with confirmations of reservations for hotels, rental cars, tours and other services.

■ Bring along telephone numbers of hotels, and other points of contact, so that you can call in the event of a change in plans. Bring along travel agent's number in case you need his help to straighten out or avoid mishaps. (See tear-out card in back of book.)

While traveling:

■ Don't be afraid to insist on the accommodations and

services you contracted for. Similarly, don't hesitate to call long distance to your travel agent when the need arises, especially if a snafu may be due to his mistake.

10. Vacation Disappointments

Before you go:

■ Try to get firsthand reports of friends or others who have visited your destination. Is it really as good as it sounds in the guidebooks or the advertisements?

■ Learn something about the culture so that you don't feel alienated or threatened by it. If possible, make an effort to learn and speak even a few phrases if the language is not your own.

■ To avoid boredom and other disappointments, make sure you know enough about the area you will be visiting. If the only attraction is the beach, is that enough to keep you happy for a week? Or do you need something else to fend off boredom?

■ Check ahead of time on the main attractions. If visiting a museum is the main goal of the trip, make sure it's not closed for repairs when you'll be there. If the goal is to eat at renowned French restaurants, consider making reservations before you leave the U.S.

■ If possible, travel to places where you have a personal contact—a friend or relative, a friend of a friend. Spending time with a local resident, or at least having one available to make recommendations and answer questions, can enrich a visit immeasurably.

While traveling:

■ Be flexible and don't give up. If the museum or the beach you were aiming for is a bust, seek out alternative diversions or destinations.

MEANWHILE, BACK HOME

Some suggestions for keeping your non-traveling life under control even if you're not there personally to control it:

Security and Safety

■ Ask friends or neighbors to check your home and while there, to water plants and do other simple, regular chores.

■ Leave a set of keys and your itinerary with a neighbor.

■ If you will be away during a period of cold weather, take steps to see that your pipes do not freeze.

■ Suspend or cancel newspaper delivery; have neighbors pick up any that slip through as well as packages left at your door.

■ Mail: make arrangements to either have post office hold it until your return, have neighbors pick it up or have it forwarded. (Keep in mind that the U.S. Postal Service will only forward first class mail.)

■ If you feel it is warranted, install alarm or other anti-crime system. At the very least, consider using a timer to turn lights on and off at pre-determined times.

- If you don't already have it, obtain adequate insurance coverage to protect you against theft, fire, water damage and other emergencies.

- Place valuables in a safe deposit box.

- Answering machine: Make sure your message does not give away your absence or suggest an empty residence.

- And of course, make sure the stove isn't on, the toilets aren't running and the faucets aren't dripping into a closed sink or tub.

Your Car

- If you don't have an assigned parking place or garage consider leaving car at a friend's home instead of on the street.

- If the car will be vulnerable, remove tape deck and anything else of value.

- Make sure locks work and car is left locked.

- For long trips, ask someone to drive it occasionally so it doesn't suffer from lack of use. (Make sure your automobile insurance will cover them and anyone else who drives your car.) Check to see if registration, inspection, parking or any other kind of stickers will expire in your absence.

Financial Matters

- Pre-pay monthly bills if they will be due in your absence or arrange for someone to mail them on specified dates.

- Make bank deposits to cover checks you will be writing.

- If you feel it may be necessary, make arrangements to call your banker or account manager from the road.

- Review your credit card balances to make sure that you will have access to adequate funds while traveling.

Long-Distance Communications

- Phone answering system: If you're on a long trip, ask someone to check your home answering machine for messages and, if warranted, relay them to you.

- If it is important for you to be able to get messages from your answering machine through remote dialing, make sure the telephones where you will be have this capability.

- If you will be traveling overseas, check on whether your long distance telephone service can be used for international calls from your destinations. Learn how to do it. Bring necessary access numbers with you.

- Will you want to communicate by mail with your home or office? If so, find out what postal service is like between the United States and where you will be. Is it reliable? How long do letters normally take from and to the States? Is the destination served by express mail? (The best source for this type of information is someone who lives or has lived there.)

- If you expect to be checking in with your office, arrange a schedule for your calls, especially if you're in a different time zone.

IF YOU STILL HAVE QUESTIONS: A LIST OF TRAVEL INFORMATION SOURCES

The systematic travel planner or frequent traveler will benefit from compiling and keeping on hand some basic sources of information.

The following section lists some publications you may want to keep in your files and some organizations that may be able to answer your additional questions. Most of the publications listed are free or available at nominal expense.

General Resources For Travel Planning

A Special Source: U.S. Government Printing Office

If you're only going to make one phone call or write one letter for additional information on international travel, make the GPO your target.

The number one source for basic information on the legal aspects of international travel by Americans, GPO also publishes many books and pamphlets that offer travel pointers or information about a particular country or language.

"Background Notes" and "Pocket Guides" to countries around the world, "The National Parks Index" and pamphlets on individual parks, and "Tips for Travelers to . . ." (nine countries and regions of the world) are only some of the many publications available from the GPO.

For a list of publications write to: Superintendent of Doc-

---

uments, U.S. Government Printing Office, Washington, DC 20402-9325 or call (202) 783-3238. In order to receive complete lists of publications, ask for these two catalogs: "U.S. Government Books: Publications for Sale" and "The Subject Bibliography Index" (SB-599), which will guide you to bibliographies on tourism and related subjects.

See Chapter Two, "Coping With Officialdom," for a list of the basic U.S. government publications you'll need to get a passport and make other preparations for an international trip.

Organizations

AIRLINE PASSENGERS OF AMERICA (AP/USA): This nonprofit membership organization represents airline passengers to the government and airline industry and offers consumer information, insurance, emergency travel services, a hotline for information on airplane flights and other benefits. For information write them at them at 4224 King Street, Alexandria, VA 22302; or call (703) 824-0505.

AMERICAN SOCIETY OF TRAVEL AGENTS (ASTA): This membership organization of travel agents and agencies publishes a number of free consumer brochures including: "Avoiding Travel Problems," "Car Rental," "Packing Tips," "Hotels: An Insider's Guide" and others. For a list of titles or to order single copies send a self-addressed stamped business envelope to ASTA Fulfillment Center, P.O. Box 23992, Washington, DC 20026-3992; call (703) 739-ASTA or check with a travel agent.

AMERICAN AUTOMOBILE ASSOCIATION: Benefits to members of the 160 federated clubs include travel information and planning as well as road services. For information, check your yellow pages for the closest local organization.

COUNCIL OF BETTER BUSINESS BUREAUS: This federation of local bureaus publishes "how-to" booklets on consumer issues such as purchasing insurance and using credit cards. Local branches monitor local businesses and assist consumers in resolving disputes. Check the yellow pages for your local branch, or write to Council of Better Business

Bureaus, 1515 Wilson Boulevard, Arlington, VA 22209.

INTERNATIONAL AIRLINE PASSENGERS ASSOCIA-TION: This organization of airline passengers represents its members to international as well as U.S. air travel policy makers. It features airport passenger lounges and financial service centers among its membership benefits. For membership information write: IAPA Dallas Service Center, P.O. Box 660074, Dallas, TX 75255-0074; or call (214) 520-1070.

The following organizations offer a range of services including supplemental insurance, emergency hotlines and information on climate and cultural conditions in particular destinations.

ACCESS AMERICA HOTLINE, a subsidiary of Blue Cross-Blue Shield, 600 Third Avenue, Box 807, New York, NY 10163. Phone (800) 521-2800.

GLOBAL ASSIST, a service for American Express members that provides pre-trip information on such matters as climate, health concerns and visa requirements. Must give card number to receive information. Phone (800) 554-2639.

INTERNATIONAL SOS ASSISTANCE, P.O. Box 11568, Philadelphia, PA 19116. Phone (800) 523-8930.

TRAVEL ASSISTANCE INTERNATIONAL, Worldwide Service, Inc., 1333 F Street NW, Washington, DC 20004. Phone (800) 821-2828.

General Publications

"AIR TRAVEL CONSUMER REPORT," a monthly score-card on the U.S. domestic airlines' records of flight delays and cancellations and baggage handling. For a copy, write to the Office of Consumer Affairs, U.S. Department of Transportation, 400 Seventh Street SW, Room 1045, Washington, DC 20590.

"AVOIDING TRAVEL PROBLEMS," a brochure, lists the red flags to watch for when evaluating a tour package or other travel offer. It offers additional advice, including how ASTA can help you resolve a dispute with your travel agent. For a copy, write ASTA Fulfillment Center, P.O. Box 23992,

Washington, DC 20026-3992.

"CONSUMER REPORTS TRAVEL LETTER," published monthly by Consumers Union of the U.S., offers information about airline clubs, hotel taxes and other consumer issues. For a subscription or back issues write: Consumer Reports Travel Letter, 256 Washington Street, Mount Vernon, NY 10553. For subscription rates and other information call (800) 525-0643.

"CONSUMER'S RESOURCE HANDBOOK," is a guide on how to complain and who to complain to. Contains lists of consumer officials of major corporations, of state and local consumer officials and organizations that may be able to help you. Available free from Consumer Information Center, Pueblo, CO 81009.

"FLY-RIGHTS," is a brochure which explains your rights as an air traveler and suggests strategies for avoiding air travel problems including overbooking and lost luggage. Available free from the Office of the Secretary of Transportation, U.S. Department of Transportation, 400 Seventh Street SW, Washington, DC 20590.

"HOW TO GET FROM THE AIRPORT TO THE CITY" will guide you to ground transportation services and fares for cities around the world. Available from Crampton Associates, Inc., P.O. Box 1214, Homewood, IL 60430. Phone is (312) 798-3710.

"LET'S TALK TRAVEL: A GLOSSARY OF TERMS," will help you decipher travel lingo such as "stopover," "shoulder," "CP," or "Continental Plan." Available free from the Institute of Certified Travel Agents, 148 Linden Street, P.O. Box 56, Wellesley, MA 02181.

"STATE AND TERRITORIAL TOURISM OFFICES," a useful resource for planning a trip anywhere within the U.S., can assist you to secure maps and other detailed information which will help you plan an itinerary. You can get the list by writing the Undersecretary for Travel and Tourism, Department of Commerce, Washington, DC 20230 or by calling (202) 377-4904.

"TIPS FOR TRAVELERS," a 25-page brochure, offers tips on a range of topics including how to choose accommodations, tipping, and special services for the handicapped, children and pets. For a single copy send $1.00 and a self-addressed stamped business envelope with 45 cents postage to the American Hotel and Motel Association, 1201 New York Avenue NW, Washington, DC 20005.

"TIPS ON RENTING A CAR" and "TIPS ON AUTOMOBILE INSURANCE" are free pamphlets available from the Council of Better Business Bureaus, Inc., 1515 Wilson Boulevard, Arlington, VA 22209.

"TRAVELING WITH YOUR CREDIT CARD" and other publications on related issues are available from BankCard Holders of America, 333 Pennsylvania Avenue SE, Washington, DC 20003.

Sources of Travel Information and Literature

Although a number of travel book stores have opened in recent years, they are concentrated in a few large cities.

Getting on the mailing list for the following mail order catalogues will give you access to maps, guidebooks and travel literature as well as planning information.

For a detailed, state-by-state listing of travel information sources see the November 1987 issue of "Consumer Reports Travel Letter," cited above.

BANANA REPUBLIC TRAVEL BOOKSTORES AND CATALOGUES, Box 7737, San Francisco, CA 94120. Phone is (800) 772-9977.

BOOK PASSAGE, 51 Tamal Vista Boulevard, Corte Madera, CA 94925. Phone is (800) 321-9785 except in California, where it's (415) 927-0960.

TRAVELER'S BOOKSTORE CATALOGUE, Traveler's Bookstore, 75 Rockefeller Plaza, 22 West 52nd Street, New York, NY 10019. Phone is (212) 664-0995.

TRAVEL BOOKS, P.O. Box 1259, Purcellville, VA 22132.

TRAVEL BOOKS UNLIMITED, 4931 Cordell Avenue, Bethesda, MD 20814. Phone is (301) 951-8533.

Special Subjects

Health
"ANTI-JET LAG DIET," available from Office of Public Affairs, Argonne National Laboratory, 9700 South Cass Avenue, Argonne, IL 60439. Send a self-addressed, stamped business size envelope. On request they will also send you a bibliography of articles about jet lag.

"HEALTH INFORMATION FOR INTERNATIONAL TRAVEL" is the basic country-by-country guide to health problems and risks. It includes recommendations on preventive measures of travelers with special needs such as pregnant women and children. Available for $4.75 from the GPO.

OVERCOMING JET LAG, by Charles Ehret and Lynne W. Scanlon (Berkeley Books, New York, NY, 1985) recommends a "total body" approach to preventing jet lag—how to regulate food intake, exercise, schedules, etc.

"SUMMARY OF HEALTH INFORMATION FOR INTERNATIONAL TRAVEL," a biweekly free newsletter, can help frequent travelers keep up with incidence of cholera, yellow fever and plague throughout the world. For a subscription, write the Quarantine Division, Centers for Disease Control, Atlanta, GA 30333.

THE JET LAG BOOK, by Don Kowet (Crown Publishers Inc., New York, NY, 1983) provides practical information with anecdotal accounts of travelers' experience with jet lag.

Packing
"HOW TO PACK YOUR SUITCASE . . . AND OTHER TRAVEL TIPS," a short book by Chris Evatt, provides advice and diagrams on subjects such as "folding, rolling and stuffing" and offers eight illustrated "packing plans." Published by Fawcett Columbine, New York, NY, 1987.

"HOW TO SELECT LUGGAGE, BUSINESS CASES AND PERSONAL LEATHER GOODS" is a free pamphlet available from the Luggage and Leather Goods Information Bureau, P.O. Box 1268, Passaic, NJ 07055.

Safety and Security

"A SAFE TRIP ABROAD" offers tips on protecting yourself and your possessions against terrorism, theft and other crimes. For a copy write the Bureau of Consular Affairs, U.S. Department of State, Washington, DC 20520.

"CRUISE SAFETY," an ASTA pamphlet, draws attention to the special safety risks of cruise travel—from slippery, wet decks to closet doors and other normally inanimate objects which become mobile in storm conditions. For a copy, write ASTA Fulfillment Center, P.O. Box 23992, Washington, DC 20026-3992.

"TRAVEL SAFETY: DON'T BE A TARGET," offers safety tips for travelers at home and abroad, in environments from subways to restaurants. Published by Uniquest, 2021 St. Estephe Court, Coeur d'Alene, ID 83814. Cost is $6.95 plus $1.00 for shipping.

"WORLD STATUS MAP," published monthly, is a graphic presentation of current State Department and other information about terrorism, war zones and other problems you might encounter while traveling. For a subscription write Earl W. May, editor, WSM Publishing Co., Box 466, Merrifield, VA 22116.

Resources for Travelers With Special Needs

Business Travelers

"FOREIGN INVESTMENTS," a GPO bibliography, lists a "Business Guide to the Near East and North Africa," "Foreign Business Practices" and other resources for business persons seeking to get involved in international trade. For a copy write the Superintendent of Documents, GPO, Washington, DC 20402 and request Subject Bibliography 275.

"FREQUENT FLYER," a monthly magazine for traveling

business executives, includes reports on frequent flyer clubs, airport facilities all over the world and international business topics. To subscribe, write Official Airline Guides, 2000 Clearwater Drive, Oak Brook, IL 60521, or call (800) 323-3532, ext. 8412.

"THE BUSINESS FLYER," a monthly newsletter, reports on the latest changes in benefits available through frequent flyer clubs. For subscription information, write "The Business Flyer," P.O. Box 276, Newton Centre, MA 02159, or call (800) 343-0664, ext. 500, except in Massachusetts, where the phone number is (800) 322-1238, ext. 3500.

RUNZHEIMER INTERNATIONAL, a management company which specializes in issues of concern to business travel planners, publishes regular and special reports on issues such as transportation and lodging. For information, write them at 555 Skokie Boulevard, Suite 245, Northbrook, IL 60062.

"RUNZHEIMER REPORTS ON TRAVEL MANAGE-MENT," a newsletter which reports on issues of interest to corporate travel planners. Write Runzheimer International, 555 Skokie Boulevard, Suite 340, Northbrook, IL 60062.

"THE TRAVEL BUSINESS MANAGER: THE CORPO-RATE TRAVEL MANAGEMENT GUIDE," is a newsletter which monitors and reports on taxes and other issues of concern to business travelers. For information write to "The Travel Business Manager," 90 West Montgomery Avenue, Suite 184, Rockville, MD 20850. Phone is (301) 424-3347.

Elderly Travelers
AMERICAN ASSOCIATION OF RETIRED PERSONS offers travel planning services and advice to its members, who must be 50 years old or over. For information write AARP at 1909 K Street NW, Washington, DC 20049 or call (202) 872-4700.

"GET UP AND GO/THE MATURE TRAVELER," is a monthly newsletter which publishes travel information for

---

"49ers plus," and even offers to match single mature travelers for hotel rooms so they can control their budgets. For subscription information write to "The Mature Traveler," P.O. Box 50820, Reno, NV 89513.

TRAVEL EASY: THE PRACTICAL GUIDE FOR PEOPLE OVER 50, by Rosalind Massow, published by the American Association of Retired Persons and Scott, Foresman and Co., Glenview, IL 60025.

"TRAVEL TIPS FOR SENIOR CITIZENS," Department of State Publication 8790, offers general information on traveling overseas as well as tips designed especially to aid the elderly traveler. Available for $1.00 from GPO.

Family Groups
GRANDTRAVEL is a tour operator which specializes in packages for grandparents and grandchildren traveling together. For information write The Ticket Counter, 6900 Wisconsin Avenue, Suite 706, Chevy Chase, MD 20815.

TRAVEL WITH YOUR CHILDREN is a resource information center which provides advice and publications on traveling with children up to 13 years old. The Center's newsletter outlines accommodations and attractions for children throughout the U.S. and the world and offers tips on such issues as how to rent or exchange homes or pack for a trip with children. For information contact the Center at 80 Eighth Avenue, New York, NY 10011. Phone is (212) 206-0688.

Handicapped Travelers
"ACCESS AMTRAK," a brochure which explains the train company's special services for elderly and handicapped travelers. Includes detailed information on facilities and dimensions of facilities on trains. For a copy, write Office of Customer Relations, Amtrak, P.O. Box 2709, Washington, DC 20031 or request one from your local Amtrak office.

"ACCESS TRAVEL" lists design features and services for the handicapped at 519 airport terminals in 62 countries.

Available free from S. James, Consumer Information Center-E, P.O. Box 100, Pueblo, CO 81002.

"DIRECTORY OF TRAVEL AGENCIES FOR THE DISABLED" lists more than 200 agencies throughout the U.S. and the world. Available for $9.95 plus $1.50 for shipping from Disability Bookshop, P.O. Box 129, Vancouver, WA 98666. Phone is (206) 694-2462.

SOCIETY FOR ADVANCEMENT OF TRAVEL FOR THE HANDICAPPED (SATH) is a nonprofit organization offering members information on travel services and publications for the disabled traveler and on tour operators who specialize in arrangements for disabled travelers. For information on SATH and a copy of its bibliography, write them at 26 Court Street, Brooklyn, NY 11242 or call (718) 858-5483. (For the hearing disabled, call (718) 625-4744.)

"THE UNITED STATES WELCOMES HANDICAPPED VISITORS," a 45-page brochure, offers guidance on a broad range of issues faced by disabled travelers, including special services offered by airlines, trains and buses, telephone service for the hearing impaired, and accommodations which cater to the handicapped traveler. It also contains a bibliography of sources for additional information. Copies of the brochure are available from the Society for Advancement of Travel for the Handicapped (see above), the U.S. Travel and Tourism Administration or Greyhound Lines. (The publishers caution that some information in this otherwise very useful book is out of date, so double-check before following it.)

Women Travelers

EASTERN'S "BUSINESSWOMAN" is a periodic newsletter which offers travel and business tips for women, including a guide to appropriate accommodations and restaurants at popular business destinations. To get on the list for a free subscription, write to Eastern Air Lines, Inc., "Businesswoman," Dept. B, Miami, FL 33148. The airline asks that you write on company letterhead and include your business title.

INDEX

Access America Hotline, 82, 137
"Access Amtrak", 143
"Access Travel", 143
Agriculture Department (USDA), 32, 33
Air Transport Association, 56
"Air Travel Consumer Report", 113, 137
Airline Passengers of America, 112, 136
Albania, 36
American Airlines, 22
American Association of Retired Persons (AARP), 42, 103, 142
American Automobile Association (AAA), 29, 42, 105, 136
American Dental Association, 80
American Express, 58, 68, 115, 137
American Heart Association, 22
American Hotel and Motel Association, 139
American Society of Travel Agents (ASTA), 17, 18, 65, 113, 118, 136, 137, 141
Amtrak, 95, 105, 143
"Anti-Jet Lag Diet", 88, 91, 140
Araoz, Daniel L., 97
"Arbitration—A National Program of Dispute Resolution", 118
Argonne National Laboratory, 86, 88, 89, 140
"A Safe Trip Abroad", 141
Australia, 43
Australian Airlines, 104
Association of Retail Travel Agents (ARTA), 17, 18
AT&T, 94
Avianca Airlines Inc., 55

Aviation Consumer Action Project, 116
"Avoiding Travel Problems", 113, 118, 136, 137

"Background Notes" (GPO series), 135
The Bahamas, 33
Banana Republic Travel Bookstores and Catalogues, 139
BankCard Holders of America (BCA), 66, 67
Better Business Bureau, 118, 121
Biderman, Amy, 63
Blue Cross and Blue Shield, 82, 137
Bolivia, 35
Book Passage, 139
Brisbane, Australia (airport), 104
British Caledonian (British Airways), 104
Burma, 28, 35
"Business Guide to the Near East and Africa", 141
"The Business Flyer", 142
"Businesswoman", 144

California Deputy Attorney General, 111
Cameroon, 28
Canada, 27, 33
Carnet, 34, 98
Carolina Losmen Hotel, 9
"Car Rental", 136
Centers for Disease Control, 76, 77, 140
Colombia, 35
Commerce Department, 38, 138
  Travel and Tourism Administration, 144
Compuserve, 20

TRAVELER'S PERSONAL DATA CARD

The following contains the only part of this book that you need take with you on your trip. It is a card that can be removed by tearing along the perforated edges.

The TRAVELER'S PERSONAL DATA CARD contains numbers and other information that could be vital to you while traveling. Should you lose your passport or airline ticket, for example, you are likely to find it much easier to replace them if you can provide their identification numbers to an embassy or airline.

Should you need additional room to list all of your vital data or should you want to include information not called for on the card, utilize the extra space provided. Also, feel free to reproduce the card for use on other trips and by traveling companions.

YOUR NAME:

HOME ADDRESS:

BUSINESS ADDRESS:

HOME PHONE: BUSINESS PHONE:

From HOW TO PLAN A SUCCESSFUL TRIP
By Ellen Hoffman

Farragut Publications Co.
2033 M Street, N.W.
Washington, D.C. 20036

Who to contact in an emergency: _____

Passport number: _____

HEALTH AND MEDICAL INFORMATION

Name of Insurance Company: _____

Policy Number: _____

Telephone Number: _____

Personal Physician: _____

Telephone Number: _____

Drug prescription information: _____

_____

Eyeglass prescription: _____

_____

Other: _____

CREDIT CARDS

Name and number: _____

Phone number for reporting loss: _____

Name and number: _____

Phone number for reporting loss: _____

Name and number: _____

Phone number for reporting loss: _____

TRAVELERS CHECKS

Type and number: _____

Phone number for reporting loss: _____

Name and number: _____

Phone number for reporting loss: _____

U.S. EMBASSIES OR CONSULATES

Address: _____

Phone Number: _____

Address: _____

Phone Number: _____

AIRLINE TICKETS

Airline issuer and number: _____

Airline issuer and number: _____

Airline issuer and number: _____

Airline issuer and number: _____

TRAVEL AGENT

Telephone Number: _____